S0-BZJ-853

# In My Father's Footprints

**William J. Turner**

MCS Media Inc.


Library of Congress Cataloging-in-Publication Data

Turner, William J.

In My Father's Footprints

ISBN 978-1-4507-0774-9

Printed in the United States of America
Sheridan Books Inc.

I would like to acknowledge the following Baby Boomers who shared their stories:

Robert Allen
Alan Augustine
Owen Ballow
Henry Bazydlo
Robert Bertoni
Bill Champion
John Dunn
Craig Galer
Nicholas Haroney
Richard Imgrund
Russ Kogut
Thomas Larder
Alfred Letizio
William LeVeque
Chris Lussier
Michael Martin
Thomas McCurry
Dan McLaughlin
Tim Merkel
Bruce Rabbitt
Tony Redente
Bob Rohrkemper
Paul Roney
Dennis Schumann
Joseph Smith
Thomas Turek
Ed Underwood
Dale Williams

My special thanks to:
Nancy Dunn, Catherine Guinan, Carolyn Hodgin and nine other readers for examining the texts, making corrections and suggestions for their improvement.

# TABLE OF CONTENTS

# INTRODUCTION

As a son and eventually as a man, I seem to have followed and grown in my father's footprints. I look upon fathers as role models to the younger generation. A father will affect his son's decisions and direction throughout his entire life. The generation which I can easily relate to is from the period which has become known as the Baby Boomers era. The term "Baby Boomer" refers to men and women born in the years following World War II and up to 1964. We, the sons and daughters of the victors of World War II, eventually became active participants in our own revolution that was the 1960s. There was a great increase in births after the war. That period encompassed both those individuals who spent their childhoods in the 1950s as well as the "Late Boomers," whose childhood experiences reflect the turbulent times after the Kennedy assassination up to and following man's first landing on the moon. The late Boomers find themselves in close affinity with what has become known as Generation X. Yet the fact that they had siblings that were more firmly a part of the early Boomer era means that they were able to share in the experiences of these older family members. The widely watched and publicized television series "Thirty Something," which aired for four years beginning in 1987, reflected the experience of the Boomer generation as it portrayed their lives during their fourth decade.

On October 15, 2007, the Social Security Administration noted that the first Baby Boomer applied for Social Security. This is significant in that it was realized that this was the beginning of the largest group that has so far applied for and will receive assistance in their retirement years. Fears still abound as to how the system will be able to provide for such a large segment of the population that is living longer and expecting to depend on this form of assistance for many years to come. For the majority of the youth in America, Boomers are either their fathers or grandfathers, and the social security payment for their retirement years will have to come from their children and grandchildren.

Today, Boomers have more resources and have experienced more change than ever before. Unfortunately, as the Boom has long ended and families no longer reflect the great numbers produced in the Boomer years, the life experience of Generations X (1965-1982) Y (1982-2001) and now Z (2002) have been greatly different. As a Boomer, I reached adulthood without digital technology. Perhaps that defines our generation in comparison to our descendants. We benefit today from the technologies that have been developed in our adulthood. The three eras that follow us, the "Echo Boomers of X" and the "Baby Busters of Y" and now generation "Z" children, whose future is just now unfolding, will benefit from a highly diverse societal and cultural environment that continues to evolve.

The following twenty-eight vignettes are the reflections and the recollections offered to me by men of the Baby Boomer era. I chose men from various ethnic and economic backgrounds who were all United States citizens. Each candidate that I interviewed was asked a series of similar questions such as what being a Baby Boomer meant to him, to relate a notable experience of his father from his formative years, to relate an experience of note in being a father, and to reflect on how he foresaw the future for him and his son. Lastly I asked if there was something he could change about his life in this era, what that would be and how could it be accomplished. Other reflections flowed from these initial questions.

I have divided this group into early, mid and late Boomers. These are stories in the experience of these men of fatherhood in the 1950s and 1960s. It is not my intention to make judgments on parental styles, or on the characteristics of good fatherhood. As a cultural anthropologist, I want you to hear their voices as I heard them speak to me. I attempted not to impose conditions or conclusions upon them. The vignettes simply tell the experience of these men and then lead you to draw your own conclusions about the experience of the age. You will read of their concerns as they grew up, their understanding of fatherhood learned in their father's footprints, and their hopes for their own sons.

As one of them, I welcome their stories, and I recognize from their experiences many elements that are part of my own story as well. As a grown son, I have found it easier to understand the energy behind my own father's parenting, and I appreciate today his work as a provider and his example as a source of discipline. Boomers shared a common desire with their fathers that preceded them. They wanted a better life for their children and they had more resources at their command to achieve that goal.

Not all would agree with the parenting decisions described, yet we all can learn what sons later recall as helpful in their upbringing. I also realize that many men do not have positive remembrances of their fathers. I have attempted to bring forward a reflective text from the voices of the men whom I have interviewed. It is my hope that men who may recall more negative experiences will be open to the possibility of understanding their own fathers from the examples of these participants.

I invite you now to listen to their voices as they relate the experiences of their unique generation.

William J. Turner, PhD, KCHS

# EARLY BOOMERS 1946-1952

The victory of the Allied troops on V.J. day brought about the subsequent return home of the soldiers, sailors, and air men who were to become the fathers of a new generation. This began a great period of family growth in the United States. There was an awareness of, and perhaps even a sense of duty to respond to, the over 418,000 fatalities of the war. These were the men of the age that were men unable to return to their homes and start families. Whether the Boomers were planned or whether nature took its course, the increase in population was a rapid one in the years immediately following the war. This is evident in the number of schools that had to be built in the early 1950s.

Early Boomers would be more likely to grow up hearing stories of a war that ended not long before they were born, although it can be noted that these stories sometimes did not come directly from their fathers. The military personnel who experienced the war seemed to want to separate themselves from the horror of war and often create a life of peace for their children. These men invariably established a home with strict discipline to which they had become accustomed in the Service and well-defined roles which they had also learned from their parents. Many of those parents were immigrants, and the fathers often exhibited a strong work ethic. The mothers were normally the homemakers, and rarely, if ever, had full time jobs outside the home. Parents stressed the importance of education for their children, supported the teachers and encouraged them to discipline their children at school as well. Parents reinforced what was learned in the school within their own home. Meals were often family affairs for both urban and suburban families, who sometimes had gardens to grow produce for meals. Baseball games were an important neighborhood event for the children, and overall there was a general sense of peace and security in the lives of early Boomers. Television came into the home in the early 1950s, but it tended to be an evening entertainment, with strictly enforced family ethics and values. Children preferred to spend their playtime outside, and the use of the television was limited. Only later did the medium become more popular when there was interest in the Cuban Missile Crisis, the Kennedy Assassination and the eventual advent of color television which added to its popularity.

The Early Boomers experienced an increase in their own numbers, which provided plenty of friends for playtime. They were often able to interrelate and be part of a family as well as belong to a neighborhood. Unlike younger Boomers, their sense of peace was not as challenged in their early years, and they benefited from the prosperity that came to the United States in the years immediately following the war. They are the Boomers who truly lived the 1950s and can reflect upon the period and its benefits when they compare it to later experiences.

## *Prodigal Fatherhood*

*As a son grows up through his teenage years he begins to express his independence. If his father has offered him good values, those values will remain with him and eventually lead him back home.*

I grew up hearing stories from my father about his experiences in World War II. He did not necessarily tell us about the heroism or even the injuries and death, rather he captured our attention with tales of the places he visited and the liberation that occurred as the troops moved through Europe. The friendships that he made with those soldiers continued throughout his life. He must have felt a great responsibility to replace the men who were lost, for we had a large family! Dad was strong in moral values, and he insisted that we express those values in our daily living. He wanted to see that we respected authority, our country and its leaders. He was disciplined in raising me. I grew up believing that this discipline was simply the way things were and that it was typical not only of his generation but also of mine. Both he and Mom were immigrants who experienced, in their youth, the struggle of entering the American society and the attempts to fit in. As they built their lives here; morals and respect were key issues in establishing their identity. That upbringing affected me and it has become important to me that my children develop a similar respect for me that I had for my father.

The recognition of my father's strengths became reality for me as I entered adulthood. He played a significant part in my teen years. When I was confused, he was able to give substance to the truth and provide a spiritual uplifting that made a difference. He had been wounded in the war and made sure that we understood that his sense of spirituality had brought him healing. He wanted to be sure that we shared in the power of that experience in case we too needed it one day. His business often led him in a direction he did not want to go, away from his family for periods of time. He then made a courageous choice for us. He announced this decision to his children and to his surprised wife over a family meal. "Everyone, I have some news. You know I have not been happy being out of town at work so much. Today I quit." Mom gasped. We just looked at each other. Out of the silence came more news. "Don't worry. I have a new job and we are all going to be involved. We are re-opening that restaurant downtown." He wanted us to be engaged together. In the years ahead we would be together in a further chapter of this family struggle to be accepted into the local community.

Through those years, Dad made the effort to spend time with each of us. He was a great counselor, always available, always accessible to communicate with us about the issues of life. I was given lessons on personal values, how to sacrifice and how to endure. I remember one instance when I was nineteen. After I had moved out of the house my friends and I had slipped into the marijuana scene. It was the time of rebellion against traditional morals. On one occasion Dad took me out for a drive saying he wanted to show me something in our church. It was a picture of the gospel story of the prodigal son. He did not accuse me of being the prodigal. He wanted me to see how loving and forgiving a father can be. Dad could talk to you without making you feel condemned even though you knew that you had done the wrong thing. He obviously loved me and this was his way of openly to welcoming me back, if I wanted that welcome. Leaving my Dad and going back to my friends, I realized that I no longer belonged with my peers. Even though it was storming outside, the rain was pouring down. I left the house and climbed the tree in the back yard. Alone amid the branches I started to cry for all that I had lost in turning away from my family. The harder the wind blew and the tree bent, the more I cried, and the more I cried the louder my father's words resounded in my head. I needed to be welcomed home.

I had to go back to school, to finish what I had begun. I had not done well at school; perhaps my self-worth issues got in the way of my studies. Dad told me that God had a plan for me. He told me to look for God's plan, not to be distracted by other things. That is the attitude I strive to instill in my children as well.

My oldest son made me proud when he decided to study to become a priest. I invested a lot of time, money and effort in making that dream come true for him. I may be living my life again through my children, but I want only their happiness and their success to be their own. Through college and then seminary, my wife and I watched with expectation of that eventual goal. In the last months before ordination, my son came home to tell us that he had chosen not to be ordained. I was more flabbergasted than angry. All those years of effort and prayer and expectation, with the prize within his grasp and, it was not right for him? What could change his mind at the last moment? My father was there again to clarify the situation for me. "You have to let him decide this," he gently told me. "You have to be the one to love and support him and welcome him home. You have not lost him, only the dream you had for him. He has made his decision and is happy to live with it." "But what will he do now?" I said. He smiled knowingly as he reflected and responded, "I understand he would like to work with you for a while." I could always use his help in my business, but never thought he would be interested in working with me. "How do you know all this?" I asked. "Because I'm your father, and he is your son," he replied. And so it was. I was a bit ashamed not to pick up on this as quickly as my father. But I was lost in my hopes and dreams and not as aware of the decisions my son would make on his own to shape his life.

I learned more that day about being 'welcomed home.' There would be improved communication and close involvement with my oldest son and my other children. I understood that you never stop being a parent and you never stop being a son. Even though I will always be an authority figure in their lives, I need my children to know I want what is the best for them. I also understand that only they have the right to decide what that "best" means.

Would I change anything about my Boomer years if I could? Looking back at the sexual revolution and the rebellion, I could do without that. Perhaps I would rather have been firm in resisting the "cultural norms" of the times. A common philosophy born during that era "I can do whatever I want without regard for the feeling of others" rings hollow with me. I believe my sons want and need to hear what I believe is right and wrong. They need to make their decisions knowing this. Even though it may be hard for me, I will now respect those decisions. I offer them my entire trust, without any restrictions placed upon my love for them. Like my father, they may see me as a black and white person in an age of a full spectrum of colors. It does not mean that they do not respect me; in fact the very opposite is true. They continue to show me they have listened and they have learned. They will remember that the welcome embraces of their father and grandfather were always there for them.

## *Special Sonship*

*The lessons a son may learn from a caring father can assist him in nurturing his own special needs son. The patience and steadfastness that is required must be learned at the hands of a patient and supportive role model.*

I never considered until now that my early life was special or unique in any way. I grew up in the country. I attended a one-room country schoolhouse with my older brother that was established for grades one through six. My parents registered me there at the early age of four, and I was accepted on a trial basis. Exposed to the example of older classmates, I did very well. At home I helped cultivate a garden on our small property. I became accustomed to fresh and canned fruits and vegetables that we all helped to produce as a family project. In those days, my father worked at a factory. He was eventually laid off and had the ingenuity to realize that with his talents he could be successful working on his own. One night, he announced at the dinner table that he intended to open a small machine shop nearby. That seemed a natural decision. Neither my mother nor my father ever made me feel that we were insecure in any way. I had no fears. There always was plenty of food, enough room to live comfortably, fresh country air, and festive, special times when my parents celebrated our birthdays and holidays. In my teenage years, I was more aware of my surroundings and experienced the various lifestyles of my friends. Only then did I realize how much my parents had done for our family with so little money. Dad had always been able to see the good in others. He was a man free from prejudice, and I grew up unexposed to conflicts over race or religion. In high school, my choice of friends was evenly distributed among the races. Early on I adopted a sound work ethic when I took over my brother's paper route. I maintained his customers proudly, continuing in his own tradition of service. As a boy scout, I was disciplined in the spirit of community service. Dad was there to help me in those days, even though he was struggling to make a success out of his new company which involved long hours and some evenings away from home. Mom was able to fill in the gaps when necessary, but Dad did not let his work prevent him from the attention we needed from him, especially on those vacation trips and regular family celebrations.

There seemed to be so much to discover in my surroundings. I remember fondly the local sand pit where my friends and I spent endless hours of fun imagining that this was our special secret place, our location for adventure.

When I developed an interest in firearms, my Dad did not recoil in fear. He felt that the usual choice of a B.B. gun could be a dangerous one, but he did approve my selection of a .22 rifle! He stipulated the condition of safety lessons at the Y.M.C.A. He then encouraged me to practice my skills in the back yard. By the time I was old enough to purchase the necessary shells for my practices. Looking back, I am amazed at how much trust he placed in me as a young teen. I remember Dad going hunting with me, but not because he enjoyed it. In fact, he was never a hunter, but he wanted to support my interest in the sport. I remember him running off into the brush attempting to send a deer in my direction, even though he never shot one himself. He simply worked hard at being a father.

I recall the first television set coming into our neighborhood and how my friends and I gathered in that home to watch "The Ed Sullivan Show" and "I Love Lucy." Television was a much smaller part of my life then. It brought to an end the days of gathering around the radio for "The Lone Ranger" and Gene Autry. We rarely spent any more time with the 78s on the record player. The advent of television marked for me the beginning of a new age and awareness of the world outside my immediate surroundings. We learned about the Atomic Bomb, the Cold War, and the race to be first in space. I recall when I realized that there were people in the world who disliked Americans and our way of life. All that talk did not really scare me. After all, there was nothing I could do about it, and there was security in knowing that Dad had constructed a shelter in the yard to protect us from tornadoes and bombs. We would be safe.

Dad taught me his ethics. He would say, "You may do some good things for others but there is no reason to go bragging about it." When we were punished he really meant it when he said, "This is going to hurt me more than you." He never used a belt or a switch, only his bare hand. It must have indeed hurt him! Although Mom was the usual disciplinarian being with us 24/7, Dad's authority was undeniable. She would occasionally threaten: "Wait until your father gets home!" That worked well, as I never wanted to do anything to upset him. One occasion he may have been angry was the night he caught my brother and me smoking in the attic. Even worse, we had taken some of his cigarettes! He quietly approached us in our hiding place and told us, "If you are going to smoke, buy your own!" I have never smoked since. Even Dad gave it up not long after. He did not always have to punish me to get his point across. I learned that I must take the responsibility for my decisions and not to submit to peer pressure.

When I was nineteen, I decided I wanted to be a police officer. Perhaps it was my interest in guns or my sense of justice, but I spent the ensuing years preparing for that choice. Policy stated that you had to be twenty-one to join the force. Realizing that a college graduate would have much more success in the profession, I went off to study, later receiving training during the race riots of the 1960s. In the Vietnam war, I served in the area of psychological operations, hoping that a police job would be mine on my return. I never regretted my choice in the twenty eight years I eventually served on the Force.

I married at thirty two, and raised a family of three daughters and a son. My son was born with birth complications, and while he survived the affliction, his development has been difficult. However, his neurological disorder and autistic traits did not prevent him from finishing high school in an assisted program. I have come to realize that his attention span is limited with the exception of outside of activities that he truly loves. He believes that I can fix anything, and I have known him to break something just so that he can have that fixing time with me. I have taught him how to drive a four wheeler and pilot a jet ski. He does both with agility and safety. It is good to see him respond with patience and understanding. In those times I, too, have learned tolerance and understanding rather than punishment for failings. My father was so tolerant of my mistakes, and I consider that as I reflect upon my son's attention span issues, or his frustration with himself over the perceived superior abilities of his friends. I have noticed that he responds to others without prejudice. I am glad to see that family tradition continue. My Dad went out of his way to participate in my activities and I will continue to strive at being that kind of father to my children.

I have occasionally considered the group home option might be a wise choice for my son. This has not been even a consideration for his mother. She has a special bond with him, and he likes and needs that one-on-one experience with her. It will be a great challenge to encourage greater independence for him. He has not been able to develop an outgoing personality outside of his family and those he knows very well. He doesn't like to think that he is different than other boys his age and often talks about when he will be able to drive his own car. While I have my doubts about how practical that might be, I have learned that limitations are often broken with enough support and attention.

Looking back, I reflect upon a happy childhood and a satisfying career. With my early retirement and a good pension, I have been able to be home more to be there for my son as he grows to adulthood. I have come to realize that I am no different than any father. Every son is a child with special needs. Perhaps most important of all is the need for a father's loving response. I thank God that I was privileged to have had such a caring father, and I will continue to pass on those privileges and advantages to this special son of mine.

## *Building Our Home*

*A talented father often astonishes his son with his abilities. His true talent is proven as he invites his son to learn from his gifts. That can be done in a variety of ways, from encouragement, to actual hands-on activity. Fathers have a key role in building their home.*

When I was in school, I remember our fourth grade teacher talking to our class about our generation. She said, "You are an experimental group and records are being kept about you as you grow." That was the first thing I heard concerning the generation eventually known as the Baby Boomers. It seemed strange that we were being singled out as different from other generations before us. Although it made me feel special to be part of a test group, I had no idea what this new age was about to bring upon us. Like many of my classmates around me, I came from a large family, and my father was under a great amount of stress to provide for us. I remember thinking how strict he was. At the same time he was dedicated and driven to see his plan for his family become successful. In retrospect, I do not regret or reflect negatively upon those days. I was part of a stable family. I was secure. I later discovered that my father had been an orphan and a ward of the State. He realized early on the meaning and importance of the hard work he would have to do, in order to be a compassionate, successful man and father.

When I was sixteen years old, I committed an act of vandalism. I knew my father would be very upset with me. I was ashamed and humiliated. The resolution of the issue went on for two years before a court date was announced. A tear comes to my eye when I see Dad standing beside me in the juvenile court room. He was there to support his son even though we were all embarrassed by my mischief and the mortification it had caused. I vowed that I would never put him in that position again. The judge ordered counseling for me so that I might work through my teenage behavioral issues. I wonder if my father thought he was to blame for my behavior. I certainly would not blame him in any way.

One of the first things that I learned from my father was steadfastness. He would often tell me, "Work until the job is done without stopping. When that is done, then do some more." Indeed, that is the way he carried out his life, his work and his many projects. He still lives that way today.

My brothers and I were always assisting Dad in his many work activities. We helped around the home or when he was active in his job of building houses. When I was ten years old he frequently took me along with him to a building site. I remember one particularly cold winter when he wrapped me up in warm blankets and told me to sit beside a barrel in which he had started a fire. From that warmer vantage point I could watch him as he continued with the construction. In later years, he would let me work side by side with him. Our family would live for twelve months in the houses he constructed, then, after the prescribed time period for selling a self-constructed home, we would move to his next project. I recall at least six times that he followed this pattern. He never put limits on the possibility of our learning a talent early.

By the time I was twelve years old, he taught me how to drive, long before I could apply for my license. Each of us acquired the skill to work with our hands and each of us had expertise in the dynamics of building a house. He would tell us, "What you think is good enough can be done even better!" That certainly was his motto as he fearlessly worked to provide a good home for us and as he encouraged us to play our part in the family's success. Our family was a success!

My mother was always in the house, cooking, cleaning and child rearing. She never seemed unhappy with her situation. I experienced peace as the order of the day.

It was not until the Cuban Missile Crisis that my happy world was threatened by a dark cloud. When the crisis was resolved, I gave a collective sigh of relief. In those early years current events did not play a large part in my life. My focus was our family. In my college years the Vietnam draft was the next threat I remember. I had no intention of going to Vietnam and I made a serious investigation into a conscientious objector status. My concerns were finally resolved when I was informed at the required physical that I was not eligible for service due to my flat feet.

I was unable to attend my graduation because it conflicted with my wedding day. Dad had just finished a four car garage at our home, with a second level as an apartment. He invited my wife and me to live there until we were able to find a home of our own. The tradition continues, as my brother is in that apartment today.

My wife seemed to be immediately pregnant; so quickly in fact that my mother wondered if she had been pregnant before the marriage! Seeing my son for the first time was a very emotional experience for me. In those days the hospital did not let you go into the delivery room to even participate, let alone record a video! I remember a nurse coming through the door and asking me, "Do you want to see your son?" As he was rolled out for me to view for the first time, a sense of urgency overcame me. I was in my early 20's, a draftsman by profession. I followed my father's lead. I had no life or health insurance, and I was now gambling with the lives of my own new family. My wife hated her part-time job and now that she had a child, she did not plan on going back to work. I could hear my father's voice telling me that I could do even better. So I went out to search for side jobs. That was the year I built an entire house on my own. I regret that I did not pass on to my sons some of those talents I learned from watching my father. Yet, they all have many talents, and I have been able to spend more time with my youngest son in recent years. A friend once told me, "Load that family of yours up and take them somewhere each year. You'll never regret it." I have attempted to do that.

I believe that I have bonded best with my youngest son on our annual canoe trips which began years ago during his scouting years. When he asked me if I was interested in the idea of canoeing, I told him I was. Although I had never been in a canoe in my life, I saw this as a great opportunity. We learned together, and it was a true adventure! On one hot and sticky July day, he and I were in our canoe when I noticed the water around us was moving fast. "Be sure to check for rocks we can't get around," I warned him. We avoided the first few obstacles, but it was not long before we crashed into a large rock, and the canoe capsized. Undeterred, we were able to turn it over, get back in and continue. This was a great lesson that we learned together. We will be together again this summer. Now that my son is nearly eighteen, he will be better equipped as a result of his experiencing an enjoyable time away with me.

I am gratified to hear that my son is very popular with his classmates. He has earned their respect by his actions. When he discovered on a class trip that one of the boys had brought a knife along, he calmly went up to him on his own initiative and said, "I hear you have a knife. Let me see it!" When the boy, who was considered a tough and sometimes volatile student, produced the weapon my son took it and told the boy, "You can have this back at the end of the trip." The other boy was left open-mouthed as my son presented the knife to an adult chaperone. While his actions make me proud, I often ask myself, "Where did he learn this stuff? I did not teach him that!"

The older boys have also not failed to amaze me. My oldest son is well on his way to a fine career as a police officer and my second son is involved in assisting stem cell research at a State university. My youngest son was the older and much healthier of fraternal twins. His sister has had to cope with Asperger's Syndrome, and even though the professionals of the day suggested that we procure an abortion, that was not an option for us. I assisted with her insulin shots and at the birth of our twins, her endocrine system returned to normal.

Today, my father is an entirely different person than the man I knew in my earlier days. He has mellowed and taken on a more gentle nature. I discovered he had been giving his resources to various charities over the years and had a deep concern for those less fortunate. He may have been taken advantage of from time to time. I know that some people owe him large amounts of money, but he does not seek them out for repayment. At ninety he dedicated his life as principle caregiver for my eighty three year old mother whose health deteriorated over the last few years. He counted on us to assist him in that responsibility, and we provided daily meals and the care until she died.

I have come to the conclusion that building a home is more about compassion and dedication than it is about wood and nails. I continue to discover the strengths of my father who has been the great builder in my life. Perhaps I should not wonder where my sons "learned all this stuff!" I hope that what I have attempted to build has also been an example for them as they begin to work at creating their own homes.

## *From Fear to Integrity*

*Does a father want his son to fear him? Respect does not come from fear, yet a son learns that there are consequences for his actions. As he continues to choose good behavior, he becomes a person of integrity.*

My father and mother were married in 1948 and had a happy marriage for forty-eight years. They were the children of immigrants, yet they managed to raise five children on a single salary. Dad was the master of the house who taught us that there were rules that we were expected to obey. I was never afraid of him, but I would fear the consequences of not obeying him. My mother cared for the home and my father always had the final say. We lived in a large five-room house on a two acre property and our parents provided us with all the necessities from Sears-catalogue-bought-clothes to plenty of food. They also offered all the encouragement needed for us to go out and find our own jobs as teenagers. We were able to earn our own money to buy extra things to make our lives even more comfortable. My brothers and sisters and I negotiated among us who would do each household chore. The only stipulation from Dad was that each of us faithfully did the work at home to which we had been assigned. I believe this interaction taught me responsibility and the give-and-take that is required in life's relationships. I often think that people today are more likely to do a task themselves or even to ignore it completely rather than finish the task in cooperation with others.

It seemed that everyone in our area had a vegetable garden. Fresh produce was available in season; we shared and swapped with our neighbors and there were more homemade cans on our shelves than the store-bought variety. In our early years we earned money from little jobs we did in the neighborhood. I was on a first name basis with all of my neighbors. Those neighbors looked out for our property and well being, and we did the same for them. Trust was the order of the day. It seemed we were more than self-sufficient in those days. We relied on our talents and the talents of our extended family and neighbors, who would lend a hand on those larger personal or community projects. I learned skills like building a house, repairing a motor and digging a ditch. These experiences made me feel more self-confident when it was my turn to do a project alone. These activities kept me occupied and out of mischief.

The 1950s were a time of personal and family financial discipline. There were no charge cards and with the exception of large items, you always paid cash. My father used to say, "If we don't have the money, we do without." That is probably why we did not have a television in our home until much later than some of our neighbors. Even when we did finally buy that Zenith, which was black and white, we considered ourselves lucky to have three channels! Of course, the networks then were family friendly. The Westerns showed us bullets that managed to shoot the gun out of the bad guy's hand, while they rarely suffered mortal injury.

My father presided over an orderly home where I knew the rules and followed them, or else! Mom was the primary disciplinarian due to her constant presence, and I did not want my father to be involved in discipline, as that meant serious consequences. I do not remember being punished unfairly; in fact, I probably got away with more and was punished less than I deserved. Classic positioning for punishment at school would involve bending over and holding your ankles as a wooden paddle made contact. For the next few days, you would be reminded of the unhappy occasion when you attempted to sit down. Sometimes my teacher would use reverse psychology. I remember one nun who would call an offending student forward to make him strike her hand with a wooden ruler. This would embarrass and humiliate us, as the entire class would see this form of punishment. Then the news would travel around the school and into the homes. My parents would not have taken kindly to the news that their son had "hit a nun." Somehow, I seemed to survive the corporal punishments and learned the lessons of the day. Growing up at that time, I learned that obedience and respect have their rewards.

My father insisted that there was a time for work and a time for play. As the school year came to its end in June, I earned money by raising and selling strawberries. He taught me a valuable lesson on work ethics one day when he saw me picking strawberries with one hand and holding my portable radio with the other. The radio was slowing down the picking progress as I twisted to get a better reception. My Dad came out into the field, ripped the radio out of my hand and threw it across the field, where it landed on hard clay and smashed. After the picking was done, I retrieved the pieces and taped the parts back together with duct tape. From that day on, I kept the radio in my pocket and did not worry so much about the reception. I had learned to improvise when necessary!

Lessons learned during my youth have influenced later decisions throughout my life. In high school, I began to consider a career in law enforcement. When I graduated from college I was able to follow my dream when I was sworn in as a special agent in the Federal Bureau of Investigation. I served for thirty-four years. I was able to meet the best and the worst that society had to offer. Social status seems to have little to do with either. The underlying personal traits lead to good or bad choices seem based on the lessons learned in early life. Family and schoolmate interaction, discipline, trust, responsibility, work ethic, commitment, confidence, caring and a sense of community were all lessons I learned as I experienced my father's parenting in the 1950s. Perhaps those simpler times were removed from the competitive world of materialism. The lessons I learned as a child and later as an F.B.I agent stress fidelity in commitments, bravery in facing the challenges of life and integrity in interaction with others.

I believe it was necessary to provide my son with what he needed, some of what he wanted, and to teach him that he must work for the rest. When he was sixteen, he wanted to play hockey. The equipment and uniforms were expensive so I told him I would split the cost with him. I did not want him to ever say that the only regret he had was not chasing his dream. "Try or you will never succeed," I told him, "Chase your dream with a vested interest in it!" I followed through with that policy when he was accepted into college. I would help him with the expense, but he would have to invest in it as well.

I believed in respect, even when fear of reaction is part of it. There were occasions I knew that my son had to realize the consequences in order to make good decisions. In my line of work, I was out of town on many occasions for short periods of time. Once when I was away, he flipped the Jeep but fortunately came away unscathed. The story he told me involved a deer and veering off the road to avoid it. It took him fifteen years to finally admit the truth that he was fish-tailing on purpose and hit a gravel patch. Respect for me had finally emerged as critical allowing him to leave his fear behind. As he now pursues a career in the finance industry, I know the lessons of fidelity and integrity will assist him as they did me. Perhaps a little fear can be a good thing, as long as fear is not a goal in itself. Everything has to be tempered with common sense. Today, more than ever, my son's survival will be based in part on the lessons he has learned and on the reminder that being vigilant is the price of freedom. As a father, I know my son will use that freedom wisely with his compass being values and guiding principles.

## ***Watching & Learning***

*A son is very proud when his friends tell him how much they respect his father. He appreciates all the more that he has such a man directing his life. Later, he realizes his own responsibility as a father and knows that his influence extends beyond his son to include others.*

I grew up in the suburbs of a large city, the oldest of three siblings and the only son. I remember my youth as a time when there were always plenty of children my age, and there was never a need to organize activities in advance. There was always something going on in which to participate. Summer was the season to play baseball, winter the season to ice skate. I enjoyed my studies; I loved to read, and I was often accused of being a bookworm. My mother was very vocal in keeping me on the straight and narrow, and she was able to manage the required discipline for the greater part of the time. My father was an electrical engineer by profession but was known as a jack of all trades. He had a workshop in the basement with a variety of tools. Hearing his footsteps descending, I would know that some project was about to begin. Whether it was a simple task in the kitchen or bedroom which my mother had urged him to complete or a more complicated creation, Dad was on the scene repairing and re-creating on a regular basis. I would watch him from afar, and I have often regretted that we did not work on those projects together.

He always had something growing in the garden. I asked him one day, "Dad, why are you planting all those vegetables?" He answered simply, "Because I really like working outside." He enjoyed growing his own food. He was a man of simple tastes. I later felt disappointed that he had never taken me aside and personally taught me these simple pleasures. How I yearned for them. The first thing I did when I purchased my own home was to plant a garden. Perhaps that garden is what made it more of a home to me.

The first concern I can remember disturbing the peace of my life was the Cuban Missile Crisis. It is especially vivid to me because of the day our teacher bluntly told us, "You people better get yourself ready. You are about to be blown off the face of the earth." I was getting ready to smile at what I thought was a joke until I realized he was serious. When I returned home that night, the news was on television and I shivered a little in the next few weeks, even though Dad told me that Kennedy was really good at bluffing and that Russian guy would never take the chance of retaliation. I thanked God that it all seemed to work out, and the country could breathe a collective sigh of relief. I never trusted Communists after that experience. Up until that time, I had never watched that much T.V. but after so much information was on television about the crisis, I became more interested in what was going on in the world. I learned quickly that my peace depended more on international events than I had realized.

I received more attention from my father than my sisters due to my involvement in sports. It was expected that fathers would attend these games, and opportunities to do so occurred frequently, in contrast to my sister's activities. When he came home, he often took me outside for a game of catch. He was a good teacher, excellent at explaining and finding the solutions to homework problems. He was available on those school nights when I needed him. His competency in mathematics made him a good tutor, and I was proud that he was also assisting my friends in the neighborhood. If the doorbell rang in the early evening hours, it would often be one of my classmates. "Your Dad home?" they would ask, and I would happily usher them in.

I have chosen to shower attention upon my sons, coaching them in sports and assisting them in their homework. Unlike my father, I have a job that calls me out of town, on occasion, for a few days. Even though I am always within the state and nearby in case of emergencies, I still call home each night to check on their progress and answer any questions that they may have.

Dad put us first. There was food on the table, a roof over our heads, special gifts for our birthdays and for Christmas and the occasional surprise. I remember the time he took us all skating. He spent so much time dressing us at the rink, putting on our skates and encouraging us to join all the others that he never had time to put on his own skates and enjoy himself. Maybe that was his enjoyment, seeing us happy and being a part of it all. He was the only one in his family to go to college. He had the book smarts and also a practical knowledge that never ceased to amaze me. Word got around our neighborhood that he had worked on the design of a satellite that was to be launched that week, and I remember the many wishes and congratulatory messages and visits he received. He had become a celebrity among us. The night of the launch we were outside cheering as Dad's satellite blinked its way across the night sky.

My father was the most even-tempered man I have ever known. He rarely raised his voice against us and never seemed to be angry. I was tremendously surprised when he was the victim of a stroke at age sixty-one and could not work after that time. I had always thought that strokes were caused by high blood pressure or too much stress, neither of which applied to him. He lived with his ailment another eighteen years. As time passed, he needed additional care. My mother suddenly died while taking care of him, and so this task fell to his children. We had grown up so dependent on him; now the roles were reversed. This responsibility came so much earlier than we had expected, but we lived day by day, knowing the duty that had fallen to us. When he died, we had no reason to feel that we had not done our best. It was our tribute to him.

Today I look at my sons and marvel. Both are in college. One is a senior the other a junior. I recognize that my older son is more like me. I watch him respond to situations just as I would have responded at his age. He is serious about his studies, earns a high grade point average and is active in sports. My younger son is also intelligent, but he is much more outgoing and active in sports. His first love is to perform on the stage and to sing. I wonder at times where they received all their abilities. Neither of them has ever been in any trouble, even though peer pressure could often have led them to drinking and drugs. My wife and I are proud parents, and we never fail to shower our attention on them both. My older son announced to me after his first year away, "Dad, I think I am going to go for my degree in engineering too." I was both surprised and pleased but a little leery. Was he doing this for my approval, or had he really made a good decision on his own? "I will be happy with whatever you choose," I told him, "as long as it is your choice, and you can see yourself happy in that field." I hope he took those words to heart. His happiness means more to me than his following in my footsteps. I pledged to talk more to him as the summer continued.

Before I was a father I had no idea of all the responsibility. If I had known before, would I have done it? I'd like to say a definitive "yes," but I am still in awe of the commitment necessary, and I am in awe of my own father for taking on such a task! I realize my son is willing to take on a greater challenge pursuing science, even though my opinion is that chemistry is not his strongest subject. Yet, I love him enough to let him decide what is best for him at this point in his life. It will indeed be a journey of discovery! I have given him encouragement in the past, always letting him participate in those little projects I had during his formative years. I hope I have been a good influence on both my boys. I know I have always tried to be. The parents of their friends and their teachers have regularly told me "how proud I must be" and "how good they are to work with," and "I hope my son grows up like them." I do recognize with pride the good men they are becoming.

I took a beer out of the refrigerator the other night and unscrewed the top as my sons watched the kitchen table, where they were talking. I indulge in a beer on a warm night perhaps once a month. My younger son said, "Dad's going to have a drink. Do you think he will get tipsy?" It would seem they have been observing me too! Even though they did not know my father before his stroke, I realize that a little good from him must have rubbed off onto me and through me onto them. Maybe it is that connection that makes all the difference!

## *Learning to Listen*

*Listening is a difficult skill. We are more encouraged to look for physical evidence rather than hear the voices that surround us. Sometimes a father must not only expect his son to listen to him but also needs to assure his son that he is listening as well.*

I grew up the oldest of four boys and have carried on my father's tradition as a father of five. Dad was an extremely "type A" person, and he was also the oldest in his family. He was the son of immigrant parents who came from Eastern Europe. My father had been a pilot in the Navy during the war. With his father's encouragement, he went back to school for his degree.

In my early years, we moved from place to place. I remember a year in California in the mid-fifties. We returned to our home state and lived first with my grandparents and then with other members of the extended family until we eventually purchased our own home. Family was important to my father, and today I have come to feel the same way that he did. My grandfather seemed a more relaxed person than my Dad. My father was serious in his pursuit of a career, and I was able to spend time listening and learning from my grandfather, whom I loved dearly.

Playtime for my brothers and me often consisted of a game of war, very popular in the late forties and early fifties. My love of family was "caught, not taught," and I tremendously enjoyed the company of my extended family and cousins and other relatives who were so much a part of my life. I was able to roam the area without fear of danger and make discoveries in the world around me. I could travel by bus into the neighboring city, walk around the downtown area, visit the Kresge store, my favorite Coin and Stamp store and occasionally go to the movies. By the time I was nine years old, I already had a "girlfriend" and had begun forming friendships that would eventually be lifelong. It was about that time that I caught rheumatic fever. This resulted in four weeks bed rest. It was obvious that my parents were worried, but I came through the experience and returned to good health. I remember the presidential election of 1956. At that time there were so many children attending my school that outdoor classroom buildings were built to meet the growing student population. Not long after, the film "Stalag 17" was in the theatres. As I watched that show, I remembered how the look of those outdoor classrooms reminded me of the stalag's buildings!

During my teenage years my father taught metallurgy at a local college. He was an engineer by trade, and was an active man who often took me on camping, skiing and bow-hunting trips. My brothers and I still get together every year to go on those trips. Occasionally, my father would react in anger to our childish ways and that seemed to be a bone of contention between my parents. My mother tended to be defensive about her sons as Dad reacted with disciplinary measures. He made a deep impression on me the few times that he asked forgiveness for reacting in that way. When I was sixteen, I remember one occasion that we were working in the basement. He told me, "Don't turn on that switch." I thought he had asked me to turn it on. When I did, and the project he was working on sparked. He reached over and slapped me forcefully. I realized that on occasion that he would be angry with me and that disturbed me. A father's anger can be devastating to his son. I kept that in mind as I watched my own sons grow and as they looked to me for an example.

I was in the army during the Vietnam war. Although my father opposed the war personally, he was proud of me. I was eventually transferred to flight school for helicopter training, and I particularly remember my leave and time home for

Christmas of 1967. I was very homesick, thinking of quitting the training. That would have meant I could have been sent to the infantry. He responded to my intention, "Don't become a quitter! It's a habit you don't want to start in life." It was more important for him that he saw me stick to my goal rather than emphasize his opposition to that war. I did decide to stay and upon graduation I was sent back to Vietnam. My mother told me that my father would pace the floor many nights worried that I would never return alive.

Upon my return I found that our relationship as father and son had changed. He did not oppose or even comment on my longer hair and my trip to roam around Europe the following year. He respected me as a person. It may be hard for fathers to see their adult sons and not remember the mischievous little one that needed to be corrected. I recall how many times I broke things or the time I dented the car. What goes around comes around, as I see my sons repeating the same behavior! A son takes the words of his father so seriously. I remember his words and have caught myself saying words like "idiot" and realizing how that must have hurt my son. I realized that my son required an apology from me. Respect is the basis of any good relationship, and I constantly remind myself to distinguish between the action and the actor.

I remember the day I was so happy with my father that I just went up to him and gave him a bear hug. Never to be one to express gestures so robustly he recoiled, "What are you doing?" After that day there was indeed more affection between us. I realized my father had felt like an outsider. That may have been both our faults. At times it must have seemed to him that life was a battle with his wife and his kids banded together against him.

My relationship with my own sons can develop friction when their independence is the issue at stake. When I had to leave for Kosovo as a Reservist for seventeen months, there was some depression and anger from the boys. My wife had to handle that on her own. I appreciated her support for them. Even though Kosovo was a negative experience for my family, it tells me volumes about the importance of a father's presence in the home.

My younger son has decided on his own initiative to go to West Point. I am proud of him, but I am concerned that he might have chosen that course to earn my approval. I tell him, "You don't need my approval. It is who you are, not what you do, that is important to me." It was not long ago that his reaction would be to snap back at me. I told him to be a friend and go over to help your buddy who needed his assistance. "I know that!" he would say in disgust. I would more gently reinforce this. "To have a friend means you go when they call you in their time of need."

My influence upon him when he was nineteen became painfully obvious to me when I yelled at him for not immediately shoveling the snow one winter. Unknown to me, he was having a crisis in his homework project, and I only made the situation worse by attacking him. When I made a son of nineteen cry, I was the one mortified by my insensitivity. Communication is critical, and I believe it to be the cause of ninety-nine percent of the world's problems. I am attempting not to add to that figure by my own mistakes. In the communications business, I am keenly aware that the specific phrases used have meaning and consequences. Relationships in life are the same. Like my Dad, I tell my kids that they should not be quitters; "Whatever you are doing, do it because you feel you need to." All my sons have grown up to be a credit to our family. My wife has helped me keep the occasional burst of anger in check, and I have been able to apologize to my sons when anger has occurred.

My wife had an insight that was an eye opener to me. She once told me, "If you tell the boys something, they might get it. If you write it down, they have it." This became evident as she noticed that our youngest son was processing experiences in a different way, correlating facts by his own methodology. I realized from this that my sons needed more than simply being told how to do something.

Neither my father nor I took the sort of time needed to teach our sons. My oldest son takes that time with his children and he realizes that there are many role models, such as teachers and coaches that can fill in the gaps for them. I wish that I had learned all of this much earlier!

My wife and I were able to be foster parents for a boy and a girl from Sudan from 2000 to 2005. Our sons were very supportive taking on older brother roles, and we were able to give them support when their own fathers were dead. It may also have helped my family to be a little more caring and observant. I recognize I have made some mistakes in parenting. My wife has been there to compensate for my mistakes, and I have been a strong support for her. I believe my sons have a very good idea of what is right and what is wrong as I have shared with them examples of discernment. I am confident that they will be able to meet the challenges of their age. They know they have a father who may not have all the answers, but a father who is always there to listen.

## *The Importance of a Father's Presence*

*It has been widely accepted that a son needs to have a male role model. The example of a father's behavior could be the first insight a son has into how he should react to his environment. A father's presence is constantly watched by those little eyes.*

My father and mother married after World War II. They came from the same neighborhood and had shared the same friends. My mother often told us that when Dad returned from the war in Europe he said that he would never return there, because "all they did was try to kill me." When he was home they immediately began to raise a family, and I was the oldest of their three sons.

My early days were spent in the city, enjoying and visiting our downtown area with my friends in a safe and nurturing environment. My father was a salesman for a soft drink company who was glad to have survived the war and to have been able to marry and raise my brothers and me. He was never a hard task master, but he expected us to fulfill our given responsibilities around the house. There was one car to take us to our various activities. As we grew older, there were four drivers for that one car. The fathers of our neighborhood were mostly veterans, who like my own father, had returned from the war and began to raise large families in small homes. Dad did not like to travel far and wide. He was satisfied to stay in our neighborhood, enjoy family life and occasionally surprise us and our neighborhood friends with free samples of his company's soft drinks. Children who lived nearby seemed to know when he was about to arrive home, and they would be conveniently present to see if there would be an extra treat available for them that afternoon.

My father was of strong German descent. Needless to say, being a German in those years only reminded people of the terrors of Nazism. As in the war years, German Americans did not feel comfortable in celebrating their heritage publicly. My mother would cook some of the specialty foods, which were always a treat, but the language was never spoken and the foods and customs that would have normally been proudly recognized as German were referred to as "our family traditions."

The progress of those days and eventual prosperity brought about the dawn of expressways, the expansion of neighborhoods on the edge of the older city, and a greater community feeling in our own region. Our area tended to be ethnic, with residents attending the same church, celebrating similar traditions. It was rightly called blue collar. Many of the fathers had jobs with the same employer.

My Dad's hobby time was spent enjoying his love of aviation. I cannot count the weekends I joined him at the fence of the airport located not far from our home. He loved to watch the planes take off and land, and he knew them all by name, where they were built, the sounds of their engines and he enjoyed sharing all that knowledge with me. I was fascinated by the science of it all, and his enthusiasm was contagious. At home he built and flew model planes. My brothers and I would chase the models for him to their point of landing and proudly return from miles away often with the plane in our arms. I clearly remember those free-flight balsa wood models with gas engines. He used to tell us with some sadness, "I learned to fly in high school and was ready to enlist in the Air Force, but they rejected my application because of my eyesight, and I was forced into the infantry." I can only imagine how his hopes and dreams were dashed by that decision. So he continued to live his love of aviation through his hobby, improving his creations up to the technology of radio- controlled planes in the later 1950s. Throughout our childhood each of his sons built at least three planes with his help and instruction. Those days and nights spent creating in our basement will always be remembered as our time of bonding. Those years were also filled with sports events, the baseball games in the vacant lot next to our house, the football games in the fall and the time we spent at the ice rink throughout the winter months. I remember him taking out the hose one winter morning to flood the property next door, so that we could have our own rink. Our area facility was always crowded. Dad also coached us in Little League. Eisenhower was re-elected in 1956, and a rage called Elvis began his career, much to my Dad's dislike for his gyrations and the new "rock'n'roll." His greatest pleasure was found in the times we celebrated holidays with his own family of five siblings. Add to his relatives my mother's five siblings and extended family, and there were the makings of a huge event.

The only crisis of any kind that I remember from my younger years was the time father's company went on strike. He was unemployed for two months. Food packages arrived courtesy of the union and government surplus. We knew things were not as they should be, but Dad immediately went out and found part-time jobs that provided for us. It was at that time that he first planted a garden in the back yard. I found out that it was a trade that he had learned while he was in the army and that he had planted victory gardens in Germany. "They forced us to learn at least one thing that we did not know how to do," he told us. "I never thought I would need to use it." Our own German garden became another family project for the next seven years.

I laugh when I remember the Yorkshire pig that my brother won at the fair one year. He brought it home, and Dad fell in love with it. I think my brother may have thought he was literally bringing home the bacon, but it turned out to be Dad's pet. It followed him around, climbed up and down the stairs and lay at his feet as he worked at his desk. He teased us by calling it his fourth son, "and a cooperative one at that," he added. Eventually, the neighbors would not tolerate him walking it down the street on a leash, and the police came and forced him to send "Chip" to a petting farm. Perhaps it was a good thing. The animal weighed 350 pounds, and my mother had her eye on it from the kitchen.

I carried on the tradition of my father in activities with my own son. My wife was a teacher and was better equipped to help him with his studies, but I tried to broaden his experience in other ways. We made trips together to Florida and to Germany. He was very self-motivated, excelling in Cub Scouts and Boy Scouts. He especially enjoyed camping trips and swimming. When I was also laid off for two months in 1986, I began painting. Friends told me I had the talent to make a living at it. With this sort of livelihood, I was able to spend more time with my son and attend more of the activities with him. Other fathers were not available in those hours, and I often found myself the only man in a sea of mothers. He was glad of the attention, and I never remember an argument or hard feeling. We had a special time working together on his Pinewood Derby project: two axles, a block of wood, four wheels and a ramp. We put it together as a team, and I proudly watched him make it to the semi-finals. I was able to share with him the beginnings of the home computer age and by 1989 we had our own computer. I taught him all the initial skills. It wasn't long before his knowledge well surpassed my own. His self-motivation has decreased my level of concern for his success. He chose neuro-science as his field of interest and earned his doctorate in Europe in 2010. We were proud when he was accepted at ten universities. He did not get a response from his application to Notre Dame. I soothed his disappointment by informing him the reason for that was "some football player had his scholarship!"

He will become a scientist. “Not the kind that does the research,” he tells me, “but the technical writing scientist.” I do not take credit for his expertise in education. I don’t push him for answers as to what the future will bring for him. I trust him to continue being motivated and successful. On the occasions that he calls me we talk about my painting, and my hobby of photography, even though he has taken it up and far surpasses my skill in that as well. He grew up so fast, and now he is gone. I wish I could spend even more time with him today. I think of my own father and wish his work had allowed him more time to be home with us. Although my Dad never went to college, he used to call me “his professor.” Maybe it was my studious nature or my nose that was constantly in a book, the eagerness to learn something new. Today, I am delighted to have my own professor, too. He is the man I am privileged to call my son.

## *Learning From My Father & My Son*

*A father cannot afford to believe that his learning is finished once he has achieved adulthood. The bigger surprise comes as he begins to learn all over again from his own son as that son matures.*

I was born at the end of World War II and can remember from a very early age how my father would talk about our lives in this country and how they had been forever changed for the better. Perhaps that is why I can sum up my experience as a Boomer: My youth was positive and forward-thinking. As the song of the late fifties would conclude, I had "High Hopes!" I grew up with confidence in authority and believed that those around me, particularly the government, were secure. The established social security system would provide in augmenting any savings we could amass for our retirement years. By the time I entered the workforce, it was becoming obvious that this "security" was not as secure as I had thought. My early retirement at fifty-five meant that I would need to go back to work to assure successful savings as rumors were in the air that the government plan would eventually collapse. I am relieved to discover that as I come close to receiving my first social security check, it seems that there will be funds for at least the short term.

My early years were filled with happy days of sports-related activities, little league baseball and trips with my father to the various games in the region. If we could not drive there for some reason, we listened on the radio. My older brother and I preferred sports to any other activity, and my father, as a former all-state football athlete was proud to see us carry on the athletic tradition into another generation. One of my greatest joys was to visit my grandmother and to ask her to take out her scrapbook with all the newspaper clippings showing my father's early years in sports. I would note that she had begun to add the news of the games in which my brother and I were now participating. This treasure was of value to me, and when she died, it was the only possession I wanted. I rejoiced when I was able to receive it. I keep it as a treasured possession today and have begun to add the accomplishments of my own grandchildren.

Knowing we were following my father's achievements and reading about them gave me something to look up to, a goal for those early years. Dad never let anything get in the way of being present for our many team sports. It became our lifestyle, the greater part of who we were as a family and the glue that bound us together. We were by no means affluent; in fact we lived in a very small two-bedroom house with the bathroom outside the building. I never thought anything of it. It simply was the way things were, and I do not remember looking around, comparing myself to others or wishing I had the possessions others had that my parents were unable to provide for me. Eventually we did move to a larger home where both my brother and I had our own rooms, but I looked upon this development as a natural progression as we grew older. My family was never focused on acquiring material things. My life was one of appreciation for what we had and the greater importance of friendship and family.

We lived in a small town near a lake, where summers were spent enjoying the company of many young people who came out of the city to augment our numbers and enjoy the recreational activities. My parents never made us feel or let us know that we had less than city families. I never remember being in need of anything; in fact I remember what we needed was always there for us. Frankly, when I heard the word "rich" I thought they were talking about me!

I remember my father taking great pains to set up my model train set in the attic, pulling the frame through the upper window as it was too large to bring through the upstairs door. I recall the many hours that were spent there in my special place and the friends I was able to invite over for hours of fun. Yes, I was indeed rich! I believe that I have grown into a man with an appreciation for all that I do have and a realization of all that I don't need for happiness in life.

My Dad also taught me the importance of getting involved in community events. His volunteerism was obvious in his school board activity and his Kiwanis membership. He was able to bring me along when carrying out his many projects.

Music was also a great part of family life. Mom and Dad organized a club for the youth in the area, which, in the absence of a high school in our town, served as the weekend gathering spot for many of the teenagers. They chaperoned the events where we learned to dance, play ping-pong and card games. On many occasions, Dad would bring in his own band, in which he played drums, so that we would have live music for those special evenings.

My father made sure that my brother and I were able to attend college and provided a place for my brother and his wife when they were first married. Mom and Dad were married over thirty years, and the first real unhappiness for us was the illness and loss of our mother. I had already left for college, but my brother and his wife were able to keep the home as normal as possible. Dad never had cooked for himself, and we often quipped that he'd burn water if he ever made the attempt. However, he was never one to waste his time, and it was not long before Dad was dating. It was too soon for what I thought was appropriate, and he took it well when I told him so. That did not stop him from finding and marrying his second wife, who would be his companion for yet another thirty years.

I would like to believe that my son benefits from my interest in his activities. Like my own father, I take a keen interest in all that he is doing. I remember when his first grade teacher told me at the end of the year that my son had been regularly disruptive in class. I was upset that I had not been informed earlier so that I could address the issue rather than finding out about it so late.

I always attended his practices, often coached his teams and made sure that as he grew he was regularly involved in interaction with his peers and with me. I did not believe in the value of idle time. I engaged both him and his twin sister in various sports and activities to see in which they would like and be able to excel. Yet, I would not push them and occasionally reminded them, “Don’t do this for me. You have to do this for yourself.” I noticed at one point that my son was not proceeding well as a wrestler. I attempted to direct him into a field in which he was more competent. “Your swimming is really progressing well,” I informed him. “Why not put your efforts into that instead of the wrestling?” But he was resolute. He loved wrestling even though it was not his talent. It was more important for him to participate and to support that team. I accepted his decision and admired him for his persistence and his loyalty.

When he began high school, we had just moved to a new home and a new school district. My insistence on knowing what was going on in my son’s life was tested as the new school did not have a travel card system of accountability in which a student would have to obtain signatures for classes and present the results to his parents. Although I could not convince the new school to begin such a policy, the teachers agreed to make it possible to continue it there at least for him. I observed in his high school years not only his continued achievement in sports, but also his choice to practice with a show choir and excel in music, too. I thoroughly enjoyed his success, and I told him so. It seemed to me that the sports and the music had been successfully passed down to another generation.

He eventually chose to become a teacher and coach in his own right. He is dedicated to those young athletes. Sometimes I worry that his own two children will miss his presence when they are old enough to begin their own activities. I told him, "If I ever am there at a practice or a game with your children and you are not, you will hear about it!" "I know I would, Dad," he told me. "Don't worry, I'll be there!"

He asked me a few years ago to be a chaperone on his trip with the class to visit Washington. I enjoyed seeing firsthand how he related to and encouraged his students. While I have always been more an "in your face" type of person as I face the ups and downs of life, I've been amazed at his ability to mediate in situations that go wrong, without a rush to judgment. I watch him as he raises his own two children, talking to them and listening as they respond. He seems to look at how situations affect all parties involved rather than only focus on the person in front of him. I muse and wonder where he picked up this wisdom. Perhaps his mother had something to do with it. Maybe as he watched my attempts at fatherhood, he has learned an even more advanced way to teach his own family the simple skills that can come from a father's love. I am proud to watch him today as he shares his love with his own children.

## ***My Journey in Discovering My Father***

*A son will often be completely oblivious to his own father's story. Upon its discovery, he understands the background and can better forgive the failings. He then becomes a better man and father himself.*

I did not grow up thinking of myself as part of the Baby Boomer generation. Such distinctions were simply not made out in the countryside of rural Connecticut in the 1950s and 1960s. My early life was spent close to home where I could be naïve about the Vietnam war reports that I heard from time to time. The news did not reach us in such an immediate fashion so common from television media today. We would hear the reports of skirmishes weeks later. I felt removed from the urgency of a war taking place so far away.

My father worked in a factory, and as the son of immigrants, he lived through the hard times of the Depression and knew the necessity and importance of working for his family. Like many of the fathers in our area, he had a eighth grade education, but that did not stop him from being a hard and successful worker. I do not remember feeling an emotional closeness to him, but I do remember knowing he was an intelligent person, able to solve our occasional problems in the family and bring stability to our home. My brother and I often experienced his strictness in discipline, and there indeed was some fear within us of displeasing the man. As his sons, we were responsible for the chickens that were raised on our five acres. This provided the extra income that was needed to supplement Dad's salary. It was our contribution to the effort, and we were expected to take that responsibility seriously. Both our parents felt the necessity of "Americanizing" their children with a work ethic that led to success in the years to come. They would not speak any language but English.

Although both Mom and Dad had a recognizable accent throughout their lives, they had no intention of letting their children be anything but Americans in every way.

From my earliest days, I expressed a love for baseball, the American pastime. My father encouraged this interest. He made it clear that if I chose the sport it would require my commitment to practice. He was not lacking in his support and presence throughout Little League, high school and even college. I cannot underestimate my appreciation for the number of times he was present at many practices and nearly all my games. I came to love baseball and was encouraged to excel upon seeing my dad, and many times my mother, in enthusiastic attendance. If we would lose, it was a disappointment to my father as well as to me.

It was not until I became an adult that I began to understand what was behind my father's great energy. I remember visiting Mom and Dad when they traveled to Florida and often had neighbors in for their infamous scrabble games. I was never much of a speller, and I saw the evenings as a fun time rather than competitive. My Dad's response to my laissez-faire attitude was an angry one. Where was this anger coming from? On a walk the following day, he finally opened up to me about his story. From that day, things would change in how I thought of him and responded to him. He told me about his early struggle when he was forced into the workplace after his father's suicide. From the day that my Dad found him and the moment he cut him down, Dad knew the direction of his life had changed forever. He and my mother were neighbors. They had eloped, and their action had caused her family to disown her. When she became pregnant, they did not feel they could care for a child and did something that was totally unacceptable in those days. All their lives they had lived with the shame of an abortion and the accusations that Mom had actually been pregnant before marriage. While I had always thought that Dad never cared about what other people thought; he had in fact been guilt-ridden and angry all those years. Their move north was a direct result of the disrespect and pressure they felt in the South. Early in the marriage, Dad contracted tuberculosis and hard times were upon the family as he was confined to a sanatorium for four years. I can understand how he must have felt locked away from the public, treated like a pariah, and the plans that he must have made over those long years to be fulfilled if he ever was released. It is no wonder he quickly found a job and never wanted anything else but the security of being a provider for his family. Looking back at his demeanor over the years, I now recognize why he never came across as a truly happy man despite the happiness which I felt in our immediate family. I discovered the truth later; he had been working for forty years at a job he really did not like. I see that as a true sacrifice of his own desires which he made out of love for his family. It is a mystery to me how he kept that fact hidden from all of us all those years.

I am certain that my experiences with Dad have shaped my fatherhood. If there was anything I wish I could have changed in my relationship with my older sons, it would be that I could have been more emotionally available to them. Like Dad, I wanted my sons to obey and do what was right, but I wish I had injected more joy into the approach. I had learned task orientation from my father, but if that is the only goal that I enforced the collateral damage would have a more negative effect than positive. I was not flexible enough. I think I have become so too late. Perhaps my image of myself as a more flexible Dad is more wishful thinking than reality. My reflection was not without its benefits however, as God gave me a second chance when another son was born years after my older boys. I determined not to hold him to the same standard.

My resolve was put to the test when my youngest entered high school. He and a friend made the mistake of breaking into a junk yard and were seen and recognized by witnesses. The owner angrily called me to report the incident and demand reparation. While my first and former reaction would have been a punitive one, that was not going to help my son or our relationship. I reflected on how my father would have responded to such an infraction in those days. I visualized his anger and distance from me for a month. It would eventually be resolved, but it would have been a very painful process. I stood in his shoes for a few moments, and it clarified how my reaction could make all the difference in this serious misstep in my son's life. A more positive learning experience could direct him to mature manhood. That is how I proceeded in this situation with him, and he has come through this test of maturity well.

My son has the opportunity to have a higher self-confidence, less baggage to carry around in his life, and the possibility of acquiring more life skills. While my father came out of an age where many did not have more than a high school education, and where for me a college education was normative, my hope for my son is a future with less fear and an education that will bring him more self-confidence and personal happiness.

It seems that this Boomer learned to change his parenting style just in time, and I believe that it was possible because I came to understand my own father better. As a result, I have therefore been able to be an even better father to my son.

# MID BOOMERS 1953-1958

The men of this period begin to feel the scientific advances affecting their lives and they often accept these improvements gratefully. They watch with enthusiasm the events that led up to man's quest to reach the moon. They are more aware of the Cold War and the threats of a nuclear age and receive the news of the danger at a very early stage of their lives. The Kennedy assassination and the age of upheaval in the 1960s have become better known to them in their wider exposure to the media. Television improves greatly and becomes the most influential medium of the times. They still only have one television, one phone in their homes, and like their immediate predecessors, watch their father go to work and their mother fulfill the role of homemaker. They are less affected by the 1950s and more so by the 1960s, and are usually part of a large family, with siblings who are often early Boomers.

Mid Boomers lived at a time when they still knew their neighbors. They accepted their parents' tendency to be thrifty, yet seemed to understand that something great was about to change their experience of society. The majority entered their teen years amid the turbulence of the 1960s, and they watched it all as younger folk, waiting to see what the benefits would be for them as they grew to adulthood.

These next short stories will express their feelings of being Boomers in the beginning of an era of change.

## *Life When a Father Dies*

*When a son loses a father early in life he is often deeply affected by the loss. When he becomes a father, he is very aware of the father and son connection that he lost long ago and takes advantage of a second chance to build a new connection.*

As the middle child in a family of seven siblings, I grew up surrounded by a lot of activity. We lived in a large city where there was always somewhere to go and something to do. I had a childhood on the run. Only as I have grown older, have I begun to understand what that was all about. One of my earliest memories was hearing my Dad come home from work. As soon as his feet hit the porch, I would run to the door announcing to the family, "Daddy's home!" It was my ritual, and it seemed that all ears in the house were attuned to it. Dad would open the door and pick me up and give me a hug for the welcome.

My joy turned into misery when my father died in 1958. I was only five years old, and I remember the day very well. I was in the first grade. Mom came to the school, gathered us all up and took us home. It was sudden, "a heart attack," she said. I remember wondering why his heart would attack him. Did this mean that he no longer would be coming home from work? Mom found a large picture of him and carefully placed it in a frame and hung it on the living room wall. For the next thirteen years that picture would represent for me his moral presence among us. I never felt he was dead. We never used that word. He was just away. That picture gave me hope that one day I'd hear him come onto the porch, and it would still be my responsibility to make sure he was welcomed back. I remember thinking, "In the meantime, I guess God is really going to have to be our father now."

Growing up without a Dad was a two-sided coin. When I saw my friends' fathers being so severe with them, I thought, "No problem, mine is dead." When I heard them talking about the generation gap, I said, "there isn't one from my perspective." Yet the other side of the coin was having no father for the father/son track team dinner and no Dad for other special moments. Even though Mom sent along my older brother, I saw it as an embarrassment that my father had to have a replacement. For me, he was forever "away." It was religion that had helped us in those days. It was a much bigger part of our lifestyle and celebrations than it seems to be today.

Eventually I would begin to believe that science would conquer the world. I had this constant reminder before me as we looked forward to reaching the moon. President Kennedy made the promise that we would be there within the decade. I remember being excited about that. This enthusiasm may have made it easier to let go of old ways and replace them with the new. It was all part of that energy, that sense of quick change for the better. However, what I experienced was something different. So many families around us were in poverty. It soon hit us as well. When I was eleven, my mother had no choice but to put us all in a boarding school. When I first heard that she had made the decision, I "went to see Dad". Standing in front of his picture, feeling as though he was looking down at me, I wanted to know what he was going to do about it. He did not have a response for me that morning, but I had one for him. I reached up, took down the picture and packed it in the suitcase Mom had prepared for me. I might not have been able to go with him, but I remember thinking, "I'll be darned if he is not going to come with me." And for the next four years he was there.

The only other picture I had of my father was the one I received from my uncle. It captured a moment of when Dad was holding me in his arms, as if he were protecting me from whatever harm was in my way. I don't remember on what occasion it was taken, but it will always be something I treasure. He was not able to play with us much in those early days because of serious health problems. Now that I look back on it, his health affected many things that happened to us as a family.

My experience as a Boomer led me to want to do things differently. "Dare to Discipline," said James Dobson. I agreed with that approach. My enthusiasm emerged in strong holiday customs, faith experiences, gardening, and even canning. I have attempted to put order into our family life today. I have discovered that each of my children has responded differently to that discipline. My second son had his share of health issues from an early age. As a newborn he nearly died from a heart defect. As time passed, he became aggressive in his relationships with adults. He did not respond well to discipline, so we changed our methods of nurturing. We soon realized that home schooling would be the answer for him. It was a good choice that began to change his life for the better.

I know that I cannot be an absentee father and expect my children to learn about fatherhood. I discovered that participating in activities with my children is critical. If I want something to be different, then I should assist in the process. I have struggled coming to terms with the way things have turned out. I must give my children the space to have their own lives and make their own mistakes. I do not have to do it alone like my mother did. I still have a loving, supportive and very present wife! I need to count on her more and let her know that I do!

I was drawn to a nursing care facility as my choice of profession. There I organized activities, and I was connected to the past through my contact with the seniors. I found that fulfilling. Yet, as I grew older and watched my children grow, I yearned to do something that would include them. I had the opportunity when I was offered some odd jobs painting. Friends had spread the word how well the boys and I had painted our home. This chance came at the right time as my son was out of work, and he jumped at the possibility. As he delightedly said, "I want to be able to work with you, Dad." It made me very proud to know that my son felt that way.

He did not realize how much this chance answered a great need in me as well. I never had the opportunity to work with my Dad. The best I could do is be there to welcome him when he returned home from work. To be able to watch my son at my side has brought the whole experience full circle. While my father was never able to see me grow into a man, I have had that privilege with my son. Perhaps I need to know that my father, my sons and I are ultimately tied together in a very special way. Is it just a Boomer thing? Perhaps not, but I experience it with my Boomer glasses on. It is interesting that I would use that particular metaphor since I have not so long ago realized my Boomer age. The age of failing sight and grunting when I try to get up from a chair is now here! It is ironic to me that my Dad never had to go through this. I wonder how he would have coped. As I look up at his picture on my living room wall, I have not lost hope that he will soon again be at the door. Each time I hear feet on the porch my father and my son come to mind. I am no longer sure that I would be able to distinguish the difference between their steps.

## *Security in a Time of Change*

*Sons remember the times when their fathers sacrificed for them. Some of the keenest memories surround that one-on-one attention. With that in mind, sons often offer the same gifts to the next generation.*

I look upon my childhood in the period following World War II as a time of real growth for this country. Even though I recognized the ominous power of the Soviet Union and the Cold War was omnipresent, I was fortunate to be born in 1957 and not be eligible for the draft during the Vietnam war. I remember an age of prosperity that included private schools, many new inventions and neighborhoods with families who knew each other and were generally on good terms with the larger community. As we entered the 1960s, it seemed we were pulled and tugged by a new age of upheaval. The hopes of the Kennedy presidency, the reality of his assassination, protests for civil rights and for peace contributed to the divide between early Baby Boomer experiences and the events that would shape my teenage years. Religious influences waned; morals, which had previously seemed black and white, shaded to grey.

Despite these external events, my parents continued to sacrifice for their children. My mother stayed home, my father went to his workplace, and their efforts provided a continuing environment of security in contrast to the changes that surrounded us. Often, my parents would make sure their older children had a vacation while Mom would stay home to look after the younger ones. My father emphasized education as the important element in our lives and took enough interest in what we were doing, leading regular discussions around the family table. Memories of those discussions have influenced my activities with my son today. I have the advantage of having lived in the same geographical area all of my life, and I have been able to keep many relationships with friends from my early years. Families nowadays are often spread over large geographic areas, making this continuity impossible. In my opinion, this is detrimental in maintaining family ties. I encourage my children to keep their relationships from different stages of their lives so those relationships can enrich their lives

I grew up in a home with one brother and four sisters. My Dad was strict with his sons; fair but tough. He believed in the necessity to "get out the belt" on occasion. I do not remember feeling that discipline was undeserved. In fact, I remember getting away with a lot more in comparison to the times I was punished for my misbehavior. We lived in the suburbs of the city, basically middle class, always surrounded by the extended family. I remember when I was ten years old my father quit his small family business. Looking back upon this time with an adult's understanding of how stressful changing jobs can be for both the employee and his family, I am surprised to think how smooth a transition this was for us as a family. Dad acted as if all was fine, and the transition into his own business never brought stress and concerns to his children. I found out later that Mom had inherited some money, and that Dad wisely handled the expenses using that inheritance. As resources became tighter and the children were older, my mother was one of the first wives in our neighborhood to work outside the home. This became a cause of embarrassment for me when the word got around. My friends would mention it and ask questions about it. At that time I didn't have answers for them. All I knew was that my mother was always careful with money and that we had no reason to worry. She never talked to us about her feelings about being a pioneer working woman. I often wonder if it was a humiliation for her. I believe that a characteristic of children born of Depression babies is the sense of being provided for carefully, that sense of planning and saving for the future now so common in funded economic programs.

The threat to our family's financial security became clearer to me when there was an accident with the family station wagon. In our neighborhood such accidents were immediately repaired. Apparently we did not have the money at the time to fix our car. Such a thing had never happened in our neighborhood. It made me aware of our situation and made me realize it was time for me to get a job so that I would not be a burden to my family. Even though many of my friends could just go to their father and ask for money, I knew that was not the way for me.

Perhaps the most vivid recollection I have of my father was when he came to pick me up at the skating rink one November afternoon. I was sixteen. For many reasons, I had used my old, tattered ice skates. I had been satisfied with keeping them in repair as that was all we could afford. As I slid into the car seat carrying my skates my father looked intently at me and said quite unexpectedly, "Let's go buy a good pair of skates for you." How I needed those skates! I knew the kind I would like to have. I'll never forget those Bauer Black Panthers, size 10 ½. I knew exactly where they were located on the shelf of the store. I sat down and delighted in trying them on. They were the best, and Dad was willing to get me the best. Those skates lasted six years, and they were the only skates I had then and through my entire college years. Only after graduation could I afford to replace them with another pair of Black Panthers. I remember talking to my father the week I finally retired those precious skates. I wanted him to know how much I appreciated them and how long they had lasted. What he had done for me back then was his way of saying that he had not been able to give me what he would have liked to give me in the past. Yet, I never felt deprived in any way. I never felt unloved or neglected. Dad had made many such sacrifices for us, simple ones that we perhaps did not realize were sacrifices at the time. It taught me that such sacrifices are not always obvious but are part of the responsibility and love that I, too, must give in parenting.

My Dad held his head high through all the financial problems he encountered over the years. Normally, we remained totally unaware and even secure despite the threat of harder times. His friends would often say that he was a man who would always pay his debts. He obviously must have borrowed but never let those debts linger. How could anyone look down on us or our situation in the face of such integrity? This was at the heart of his example to others and to me. I realize today what I have learned from his way of life. The primary thing is to be a man of character when dealing with situations that come your way in life. As I raise my family, I realize that I may or may not have all the resources I need to do what I want to at this particular time. More important than resources, however, is to know the right thing to do at this moment. I pledged to raise a family with character and integrity and not to be held back by the thoughts of what other people might think.

As I consider my son and how I attempt to raise him, I cannot help but think about my father and those skates. I have been able to give my son much more in gifts and conveniences than my father provided for me. It has seemed natural in the twenty-first century to have more and give more. I decided to celebrate the memory of my greatest birthday present on my son's sixteenth birthday. His greatest hope was to own a Hyundai Tiburon. While I would have formerly considered such a gift extravagant, I recognized that car was just as important to him as those skates were to me. His whole life recently had revolved around the love of cars and engines. This car is not only his future transportation; it is his passion. It was my way in sharing in his love for cars even though I do not share his enthusiasm for them. His reaction was to tell me he felt as if he had "died and gone to heaven." As I watch him carefully preserve the finish and proceed with the detailing, I am sure he has been given the encouragement and support he needs today as he celebrates his talents. I hope his experience will make him thankful as I was. I hope he will be all the more willing to one day pass on to his son the security that comes from the support of a father who loves him.

## *Education, Work & Alcohol*

*Sometimes even the negative behavior of a father can instill good values in an observant son. Such a son can break the chain of dysfunction, raise a healthy family and even assist in his own father's recovery.*

When I think of what it means to be a Baby Boomer, I think of the fact that I will not be able to receive Social Security payments until I am sixty six or sixty seven! I have been instilled with the same work ethic as my parents, including loyalty to my company and to my family. This age has provided a much better lifestyle for me so far as compared to what I remember as a child, but I often ask myself, "What will it be like for my sons? Will there be enough for them and will the pot of prosperity continue indefinitely?" My father took stock in education as the necessary direction for his boys. He was determined that we should all go to college, and he made sure that happened for each one of us. Perhaps as a direct result of the effects of World War II, I benefited from an age of growth not only in a population boom but also a great technology boom. There was a sense of newness all around me, always a new invention or a new product to benefit my young life. I would eventually be in that section of Boomers who would miss the Vietnam war draft and were lucky enough not to know or really understand the horrors of the war or the earlier ravages of the Great Depression. My parents, on the other hand, lived through and were affected by both these negative experiences.

My father's career was in international business, and his family soon took on that international flavor as we travelled overseas and were schooled in other countries. The 1960s were great years to study abroad. A sense of individuality abounded and there was an openness for new things and new people. This international education has had its effects on how I function in the global business world today. I had no doubt that the benefits which I received were all made possible by my father's energy, enthusiasm and work ethic. As a C.P.A., he had many professional connections that only increased with the passing of time and with the many countries to which his work directed him.

The earliest memories I have of my father's purposefulness and direction is of annual trips to the Jersey shore. He would rent a house there, and we would spend a happy time as a family together. He seemed to leave behind the pressures of his work to dedicate some time to us. I remember one occasion that Mom and Dad were sitting on the front porch while we played on the front lawn. I was about six years old that summer. A rather rough looking character on a motorcycle zoomed by amid a cloud of dust and gravel which struck us as we sat on the ground. Dad immediately reacted at seeing the danger we were in. He screamed after him, "You careless idiot! What do you think you are doing?" The man obviously heard what he had said, brought the motorcycle to a halt, turned around and slowly drove back to face his accuser. He set aside his bike and grabbed a chain and came menacingly at my father while all of us watched in horror. That concern turned to pride as we watched our father deck him with two swings. I had never seen him react violently before, but I learned that day that he would always be there to protect us. I felt safe after that. I asked my mother, "How did he do that?" She was able to tell me that of which he never spoke, his time as an infantryman in World War II. He had been a prisoner of war for nearly two years, liberated by the Russians and hidden by the Polish. My father never talked about those years and I sense this is similar to many fathers of the era, who, for whatever reason, put the experience behind them and did not pass those stories onto their sons. I remember my father often saying, "I don't sweat the small stuff." While I always respected that and understood the good lesson from it, only later did I appreciate the experience that brought about that wisdom.

My work and travel parallel my father's experience in many ways. I reflected on those times away from my family as to how I could encourage my own twin sons when I finally returned home. I decided on the importance of a "man's outing" with the boys, trips to Utah where I would teach them skiing. My wife told me that one of their responses to this was, "Wow! Dad is a great skier!" Like me, they were surprised to find out something their Dad could do that they had never discovered. They still talk about those trips today and I am grateful to have been there for them.

Being a father is about being an example. I think that a younger father should be patient but a little stern, easing as a son grows older. I have often considered the great responsibility to raise, provide and counsel one's son about everything, including difficult topics like sex and drugs. My hope is that faith and their religion will help them as they grow older. As I have a daughter as well, I have noticed the different skills required to bond with her. The fact that there are many accepted and acceptable rituals and activities makes the relationship of father to sons more natural to me. But whether it is son or daughter, I think what I can do best as a man is to instill values I feel are important. My father seemed to be aloof at times. This has created in me the desire for closeness. I want my sons to come to me, and I freely make known to them my unconditional love for them. "Never be afraid to tell me what you have done." I have reinforced this in them and did so especially during their teenage years. I was somewhat fearful of the standards my father set up for me. Sometimes, just considering his expectations for my behavior was enough to create dread. I am proud to say that my boys think I am a great Dad, but I wonder if I there is not a distinction to be made between father and parent.

That distinction is revealed in another aspect of my Dad that emerged as we grew older. When we eventually returned to the United States, Dad discovered that he did not like his new job, and he began to drink as a solution to his dissatisfaction. When I was sixteen, I remember him insisting his sons have crew cuts, and he seemed to be less generous in our allowance and with our requests. His drinking may have only increased as I later discovered that he had lost a great amount of money in his stock market investments. Although he never struck me, he became abusive in an authoritarian approach which reflected his military background. He detested the 70's, a time he called "liberal arts, rock 'n' roll and drugs." As I was part of the generation that he was attacking, his reaction was not particularly a happy one. Although I never doubted his love as a father, he seemed to grow more and more unable to show it.

Dad retired when he was fifty five and decided to move south to a warmer climate. Distance precluded the family being together in those years. For the next thirteen years the family seemed to drift apart, as we had grown and eventually married to begin families of our own. Mom's diagnosis with cancer and her death deeply impacted his sense of well being; his drinking increased more and more. My brothers did not want to accept this downward spiral as they had already experienced the agony of Mom's death. I, as the oldest son, was the one to enforce the reality check. I set up an intervention where we all were together. Dad decided that drink was all he had, and drink was what he was going to do until it killed him. His only promise to us was that just as he had paid for our education, he would leave us money when he died. He fulfilled that promise when he succumbed to his illness less than two years later at age seventy-five. I was angry about his decision to die because to me he had become comfortable in accepting alcohol-related suicide. I am sorry that my sons will only remember him in those alcoholic years. Despite that negative experience, and because of their happy family life in our home, they will be good fathers. The older twin will have my Dad's capacity of loyalty and stability, while the younger has more of what I see and love in his mother's strengths of being organized and driven. My wish for them both is the happiness that comes from knowing their father loves them and supports them and that neither work nor anything else will prevent them from giving all the time and attention their children will need. How much I look forward to seeing their families grow!

## *The Value of Truth & Integrity*

*A true man and father is willing to admit when he has made a mistake. He knows the value of the truth and instills that value in his son. He realizes that an admission of fault is not weakness, but strength.*

I have lived in an age of security in financial matters and prosperity after World War II, but our security did not prevent our family from enjoying moments of delightful spontaneity. On many occasions my father would come home from a day's of work and announce then and there that we were headed off to the lake. These trips were never planned but rather out of the joy of the moment. Those days were days of flourishing small towns and countryside, free of the eventual urban sprawl. My usual play place was the surrounding woods, and my best friend was the son of a park ranger. Free from the earlier age of our parents and grandparents with its economic hardship, my days were spent in a form of superficiality. I had a happy childhood with occasional surprises in the new creations of consumer products and modern technology. I remember the "new and improved" age or at least we were led to believe the new things were actually an improvement! My father's lessons to me often bolstered my moral character, encouraging me to be a trustworthy person and his firm belief that a lie was the greatest sin a man could commit. I clearly remember his instruction to me, "I don't care what you have done, how bad you think it is or how angry you might feel I will be, tell me about it so I can help you then and there. Don't ever lie to me! It will be easier on you if you tell me up front what happened." His promise was put to the test not long after when a friend and I were playing and noticed a sign that said, "Water Over the Road." It struck us as so funny, since the road was dry, and we thought it would be great to take that sign and show it to our friends. Unfortunately, we were seen and followed by an off-duty policeman. It was bad luck for me! He followed us to my friend's house, where later the police appeared at the door, after I had returned home. Unknown to me, my friend told of my involvement and within the week, a letter from the prosecutor was sent to our home. My father called me into his room that night and, pointing to the letter on his dresser said, "Any idea why I would be receiving a letter from the town prosecutor?" Wisely, I immediately told him the story. My Dad had a sense of humor, but if I had lied and not come clean, it would indeed have been much worse for me. His tone was "how we are going to address this" and "have you learned a lesson from this?" rather than threats of punishment. We were fortunate to live in a town where these things were handled between the parents and a supportive police department. The next day on the way to school, a police car pulled up beside me. The officer yelled out his window at me, "So, I hear you will be doing community service for your shenanigans!" He smiled broadly as he rolled up the window and sped off.

As the second of five children and the first son, there was some sibling rivalry among us. I remember one occasion when I was seven. My sister got back at me by telling my father that I had broken her favorite toy. My father took no time in reacting to this perceived disrespect for property. "Did you break it?" he asked me. "No, Dad, I know nothing about it," I gulped. He took off his belt and bent me over for a good strapping. "Tell the truth," he said. "I didn't; I didn't touch it," I wailed. "Apologize to your sister," he demanded. "No, I didn't do it," I screamed. He looked up and saw my sister smirking in the doorway, and his expression softened as he began to realize he had been tricked. Dropping his belt he held me close and apologized over and over for the mistake and the injustice of it. "What I did was wrong in not believing you," he lamented. "Will you forgive me?" It made me feel so good that my father respected me as a person instead of a child or a possession. It was good to know my father accepted that I knew right from wrong and how to choose the right.

I made a serious mistake three years later. Again, it was with my sister. She still seemed to want to establish her seniority over me. My brother and I would come home as early as possible on certain weekdays to enjoy watching the monster or cowboy movies that were on T.V. We also enjoyed our roughhousing during the commercials. It had been my responsibility to empty trashcans. For some reason on that day I had forgotten hers. She wanted it emptied now, and I put her off. Entering the living room she proceeded to empty the basket on my head. Reacting angrily, I jumped up and hit her across the mouth. She went off crying into her bedroom. It was reported the moment my father arrived home. He came into my room and questioned me, "Did you hit her?" "Yes, she threw her garbage all over me." Dad grabbed me by the shirt, took firm hold so I could not get away and was directly in my face. I was more embarrassed than hurt. "How dare you hit your sister," he growled. "A man never touches a woman, ever!" He was definite and to the point and shook me as he spoke. "You will never touch a woman again. That is the worst kind of man." My father knew what he was talking about. Around our neighborhood there were often reports of men beating their wives and this upset him greatly. When he believed that I had hit my sister he was determined to teach me what I never would forget.

My son is in a much better environment today. I was more of a mouthy kid and was rightly disciplined on occasion. He is different than I, more aware of those around him. We have developed a close relationship over the years, during trips to Canada fishing for brook trout. Sitting in the boat my son would never stop talking about growing up, taking responsibility, girls, and what it means to be a good and trustworthy person. He grew up in a house of older sisters. Thinking back over my experiences I assured him that we have something in common! Yet, while I was the kind of person to jump into the lake before I check the depth, he is more conservative, reserved, and cautious. My frustration at his tendencies was made evident when I tried to teach him to ride a bicycle. He was reticent to let go of that fear and pedal! The worst came out in me when I called him a sissy. I still pay the price for that outburst when my children just look at my frustrations knowingly to say, "There he goes again!" or "Dad does not handle teaching the bicycle well!" My oldest daughter came to the rescue, and I thank God she is a person with patience and control over her frustration level. I have come to realize that sometimes I help my son better by not helping him. I told him, "I'm not good at everything, you know!" His eyes widened when I said that. And like my Dad, I apologized to him. "You are not a sissy," I recanted, "just more cautious than I. I need to work on my patience." I meant that, and it was a lesson I learned from my son.

I always encouraged my son to abide by the rules. I reflected upon this wisdom when I found out that a bully had been punching him at school, and he had refused to fight back in accordance with the school rules. I told him he had my permission to defend himself. The next day he came home smiling, "I don't think he will be punching me any more Dad! I told him that you had given me permission, and I slugged him back!" "What happened then?" I asked. "We decided not to fight and to become friends," he shrugged as he walked away. I did not need to ask any more details. He has since gone off on his own to earn a black belt in karate. He is known around the school as the boy who will defend the underdog. In our own neighborhood he has been the only friend to a troubled boy who was kicked out of high school and seemingly had nowhere to go for advice. It is fortunate for this boy that he has found a loyal friend, one who will even bring him to his own Dad for advice. I don't know how much I can help, but I never cease to be amazed at the purposefulness of my son as he refuses to give up in a seemingly hopeless situation without first bringing some encouragement to those around him.

I am closer to my son than my Dad was to me. Not that I did not spend time with him, but we did not have the same quality talking time. I wish I could slow down the pace of this new century. There seems to be fewer playtimes to enjoy the simple things, the natural things in life. I miss the times that we had to build the rafts, to play in the tree houses, to create forts. Amid all these fast-paced activities and demands on our time, there is no time to explore the world with my son, something I always dreamed of being able to do. While our children do not seem damaged by not enjoying the carefree childhood and adolescence I had envisioned for them, I would like to think that they would be free to spend some quality time with me. Sometimes it seems I need to make an appointment!

My hope for my son is that he will be free from the world's current focus on success and be able to celebrate the happiness that comes from all that is good in family life. I am proud that values of truth and integrity have indeed been passed on!

## *Making the Effort Together*

*Fathers and sons grow closer as they work together in a common project and meet success as a team. Perhaps it is in the very art of supporting one another that they come to realize what is best in their relationship.*

While I was growing up in the 1950s, I never felt the significance of what has become known as the Boomer generation. I accepted the times for whatever they were and lived day by day, enjoying my experiences. Looking back upon those times, I realize that it was an innovative age, yet I did not focus so intently on what was new and revel in it as seems to be the case with the children of today. For example, I remember our first television. It certainly was new and innovative, but we did not spend excessive amounts of time sitting in front of it, casting aside the activities in which we participated in favor of this tremendous invention. True enough, there were only a few channels, as opposed to the two hundred I have today on my satellite dish. Even as I roll through the current channel listings, I am hard-pressed to find a program that I find fascinatingly engaging. My father was particular about what we watched, and I had a definite sense of his supervision and interest in what this new media presented to his family. Compared to today, the quality of programming was for the most part wholesome and family-friendly. Since news arrived at a much slower pace, it could be refined in such a way that the news often was available with a conclusion to the story rather than the viewer being left in a state of stress, waiting for the solution to be reported at some later date.

My childhood was similar to the experience of other children around me. Dad went to work; Mom stayed at home, and I walked to and from school as there was one car per family.

As the economic situation improved through the 1950s, we were able to have more conveniences provided by the emerging technology. Once this trend started, it seemed that there was no turning back. Although I feel that these improvements were great things and indeed the genius of our age, I compare it to a child who is spoiled by too much all at once, and is overwhelmed by the experience. Today I have watched my son spend hours on the telephone. He carries his cell phone everywhere he goes. My home had one phone, and it was considered for important business, where talk was kept to a minimum. Sometimes the line had to be freed for another party who shared it. The downside of the great buffet of choices placed before us today is the focus on all of that "food" as a normative factor, rather than a contributive factor to our overall health. Yet, I do not yearn to return to another age as a solution. A goal in our age would be to work on encouraging family life which has been lost amid all the distractions.

I am tempted to compare the school curriculum today with the method of study when I was my son's age. I remember learning math in a particular way, memorizing times tables and the disciplines of calculation. The modern methodologies have abandoned the former techniques, yet my son, who would more likely use a calculator than figure sums himself, seems to have discovered new ways to find the answers. However, I find it sad that we seem to be encouraged to rely more on things than to rely on each other. As I notice people focusing more on their possessions and constrained by their busy schedules, I do remember the times of my youth, free from many of the so-called advantages that technology provides. You can do everything on-line today. There is no necessity of a personal contact, no real reason to leave your house. When people were communicating face to face, you knew your neighbors because they were your way of connecting, and there was no technological replacement for them. I never cease to be appalled by the encouragement we receive from ads to go on-line to send your condolences to a funeral home rather than "have to visit," or by suggestions to mail your wedding gift directly so you can "save the bother" of presenting it at the wedding. It seems that new technology wants to "save us the problem" of having to associate with other living, breathing human beings. These extra devices could have helped our communication skills rather than prevent us from truly communicating with others. Rather, they seem to call us to avoid any interactivity. For example, the computer and a web cam have made it possible for me to call my children and see the live images of my grandchildren who live across the country, virtually free of charge. This advantage is not a replacement for seeing them face to face, but is a modern day invention that makes the time between visits seem not as long.

My father was a "totally committed to getting the job done" guy. He took his work seriously and was never known to take a sick day or be late. He made his choices in life, and I watched him adhere to those choices. I remember him as a fine example for his sons. One of my early memories of him was our sailing trips where he showed me the skills and the fun of sailing, a hobby I enjoy to this day. He was somewhat of a perfectionist, and I had difficulty measuring up to his expectations. I proudly accepted his request of me when, after we moved into a new home, he asked me to be his "helper" in refinishing the basement. I had to learn quickly about the types of tools, what function each could perform and how to use each one safely.

The benefits of my father's ingenuity were obvious. As the first of four children and his oldest son, I was perhaps more able to compare our affluence to the families with whom we associated. If our friends came over with a new toy, and we expressed the desire for it, my Dad would respond, "I can't afford to buy you that, but I can make you one just like it." Often, as it turned out, our friends would rather play with our home-made reproduction than the original. "Let's use yours!" I remember my friends saying on more than one occasion.

I was proud of my Dad. He was more than the man who provided for us or the adult who once in a while defended us against the neighborhood bully or as the tough disciplinarian. He was all those things, but he chose to express his love for us in actions and that made our years of growing up so much happier. I can say with the deepest affection that I love the man to this day. I was happy to know that Dad had provided even more for our family as the years passed. He was indeed rewarded, as was our family, in the economic upswing. Today my parents can retire in comfort and enjoy their remaining years with security.

I am happy to know that my older son has always felt able to call on me for advice and support. Our proudest moment together was when he organized a rather complex Eagle Scout project. I encouraged his efforts through the ups and downs to completion of the work. It was totally his plan and his conception. While he counted on the support of his mother and me, we were proud to see his efforts reach completion.

My younger son had a hard act to follow in his project, which he chose as a continuation of his brother's efforts, but he also was able to succeed. It is hard for me not to compare the two of them, but I encouraged both of them to set a goal and to do all in their power to be successful.

I am happy today to be the father of two Eagle Scouts! I never had the opportunity to finish college, but I do not want either of my sons to think that, even though I am successful, they can expect the same success without a college education, so critical in this age. "Working with your hands can be a risky vocation," I tell them, "especially if there is no education to fall back on when those hands fail you."

Throughout their lives I have encouraged them in following the family tradition of sailing. My interest in the sport was more that of a racer than a sailor. I do not think my father understood this emphasis on my part. He liked to be the skipper, telling his mate how to proceed. While I followed his direction, that method limited my real ambition to do the tasks I had in mind. I am a man who is not satisfied in being on the bottom of the totem pole. I would not encourage my sons to be satisfied there either. I remember how I struggled to please my father, and I hope they have had less of a struggle to satisfy the need to please me. I wonder if all fathers and sons go through that. Recently, I watched my son cut the lawn, mentally noting that he missed a few edges. Do I tell him that he missed something or praise the effort? I've decided to make sure he continues to get the necessary encouragement. After his task he came inside to say: "What do you think of the lawn, Dad?" He asked me that rather sheepishly. I immediately responded, "If you don't get that summer job, and I hope you do, it won't be for a lack of ability on your part!"

Boomer fathers may have been somewhat reluctant to share their feelings about being a father. Because I was able to recognize my mistakes in fathering and, at times, admit them to my son, I have no regrets. Our sailing together characterizes our relationship. He has told me: "I'd rather race with you than anyone else," and "The boat goes faster when you drive it!" "We'll go even faster if you help," I tell him, and as father and son we make the effort together.

## *Minding My Father's Business*

*A son sometimes has the opportunity to live out the dream of his father, to follow in his footprints. As he respects his heritage and traditions, a son can keep alive not only his father's business, but the best of all that is family.*

I recall my early years as a time when my father worked hard to provide for his family, a time when there was not a lot of extra money to be extravagant. We lived a simple but comfortable life in a home prepared by my mother, from whose domestic abilities we all benefited. Dad worked long days, and my earliest memories surround my brothers and me in nursery school. Our early education was in the small town in which we lived and later in a country setting, where I watched out the window as trains went by across a large expanse of fields. All of us had the opportunity to attend a local private school, but as I later struggled with my studies in those early years, my parents decided to accept the advice of my teachers and to transfer me into the public system. There I seemed to fit in better, but I never excelled in studies until my college years. My early years were filled with family times enjoying the benefits of a small town, where a heritage from my great grandparents provided a large extended family and where our family name was well known and respected. Family celebrations were regularly held during the holidays and especially at Christmas time. These are my earliest memories of my father as the enabler of special family times. We shared our family history, and we surrounded my grandfather as the patriarch of new generations which he was proud to lead. Dad worked for his father in our family business. As his sons grew, we continued the family tradition. Because I was more interested than my brothers, from an early age I was the son most interested in a future in which I played a key role in the business. I first worked in the hardware store when I was eight years old. In my teenage years I became a more regular part of the operation, where my father and grandfather and great uncle certainly had an impact on me. Later, my father began to run the company, in preparation for what would become his inheritance in partnership with his brother.

However, my whole life did not revolve around work. Like many a boy in those days, I enjoyed the recreation available in a small town. We enjoyed baseball, creating tree forts and fox holes, riding my bike to our local dime store, watching black and white cartoons on the television. It was a rare occasion when I was unable to find a neighborhood child who wanted to go outside to play when the time became available.

School and T.V. gave me my first awareness of the outside world. I heard that the Russians were Communists and therefore the "bad guys" and that Khrushchev was their leader. We were the "good guys" in the effort to defeat the menace. The world lined up not unlike the cowboys I had seen on T.V., white hats representing the good and black hats representing the bad. It was not long until we had a series of national shocks, beginning with the assassination of the President. I was told that we would always remember where we were and what we were doing when we first heard that news. It was a rainy Friday, and we could not go outside for recess as usual. The teacher was called out of the classroom. When she returned, she told us President Kennedy was dead. It seemed to me that this news was first in a series of events that taught me that American society could be a dangerous and violent place. The eventual assassinations of Robert Kennedy, Martin Luther King and the ensuing race riots changed the world I knew, even though I was never in close proximity to the violence I had watched on T.V.

I was fortunate to not be a candidate for the draft during the Vietnam war. I learned from overhearing my parent's conversations the belief that, unlike wars we had fought before, this war was not morally justified. The reported protests and civil disobedience reinforced their viewpoint in my teenage mind. I was too young to be a part of the hippy generation of the 1960s, but I remember it clearly, as well as the misuse of drugs, the rejection of traditional sexual values and the loud anti-establishment voices. I have heard it described as an age where young people lived together before marriage, didn't believe in God, disliked the government and did not respect their parents. That may be harsh and stereotypical, but it was my experience of the emphasis of the age that was upon us. The 1950s were a happy time of life in the care of my family, while the 1960s brought forth a turbulent, idealistic, emotional, energy-filled coming of age. Although the values of peace and love were vocalized by the youth, I later came to realize that many did not truly understand those virtues and often succumbed to the excesses around them.

My first memories of my father were of his great smile and his playfulness when he returned home from work, the horseplay, the wrestling and playing catch in the back yard. He was home at night on most workdays, and we gathered around the kitchen table for meals and talked about our lives. I was fortunate that my parents had a caring and loving relationship. Although with five children his time was divided among us, nonetheless Dad was able to give me the attention I needed in such projects as my soap box derby. He helped me with the construction, and I remember how greatly I appreciated that.

I soon realized that our family business was much akin to the family farm experience from which we all descended. It would become for my father as it did for my grandfather, an assured retirement plan for his later years. I was grateful for the opportunity to work there. In 1980, after my years of college that led to a short stint in a job away from home, my father called to say that he needed me and offered me a position explaining that a vacancy had occurred. I immediately jumped at the chance to return to a more family-oriented life. Dad handled the administration of the business while my uncle took care of the purchasing and sales division. My tasks were installations and customer service. I was married shortly after and began to raise my own family. By 1992, I was able to begin the process to move to ownership myself. My father was ready to move toward his retirement years, yet he assisted in the transfer process until 2000. Even though he had purchased the business from my grandfather, his father stayed and worked there until 1982. My Dad had no intention of repeating that as part of the family tradition. He made a clean break, yet was always available if I needed advice. He continues to encourage me with his interest today while enjoying a well-deserved opportunity to travel, enjoy his grandchildren, and of course, smile. He has been a patient, loving and communicative father who has told me that he loves me. I have not failed to count my blessings for the gift of good parents.

I am proud that both my sons will be college graduates soon. My father taught me to be direct and I have been so throughout their lives. I believe in looking them straight in the eye when I talk to them. Although my wife has traditionally been the disciplinarian and I more of a trump card kept in reserve for back-up, I have had my share of using parental skills. A son will often attempt to test the limits of the rules, and I have had to say a firm "no" on occasions. Whether it was the attempt to stay out longer than was my policy or trying to convince me of the practicality for a trip out of town on a school night, I reflect on this as a payback time for what my Dad experienced from me. "Do I let them go free? How much do I deny them?" I learned that communication and communication skills play a large part in the solution to such parental dilemmas. One occasion that brought this forward vividly was my son's intention to spend the summer overseas with his girlfriend. I convinced him that "no" was a wise response and he came to accept that decision. My own father was strong enough to express clearly to me his belief on what was right and what was definitely wrong, even though I may have disagreed at the time. He was a man of principles who attempted to pass those principles on to me, and I have continued in that good tradition.

My sons worked in the business a little during their teenage years, but I do not expect them to choose it as their life's work in the years ahead. As my father had five sons each of whom had many children, I am confident the business and the tradition will survive. My sons have skills that are not necessarily business oriented. Although I admit to originally having the secret wish that they would join me one day, their freedom to choose for themselves is more important to me.

I believe that I have been a good role model as father for them. I continue to be concerned about their lives and careers, and they know I am willing to assist them. I want my sons to follow passionately on that path towards their eventual success. Life for them should not just be about a career, but rather the life choices that lead to happiness and fulfillment. In a few short years, I will have completely paid off the business debt to my father. I never will be able to pay the real debt I owe him. I want to be that same kind of father, strong enough to tell my sons I love them and man enough to allow them to make their own choices in life, choices made easier by the unyielding power of a father's love.

## *Adopting Duty*

*Fatherhood is not restrained by biology. An adoptive father becomes a father in every way as he raises his son and teaches him the life lessons that were passed onto him. Such a man truly has earned his name as "Dad."*

My childhood memories are quite vivid. I recall moments like John Glenn travelling into space, the Kennedy assassination and the night the Beatles were on the Ed Sullivan Show. I would not want to diminish the other events, but I was a huge fan of the Beatles, and that night was a shining moment for me. I recall the day my favorite team won the World Series, and I remember experiencing an age when social and political upheaval were reactions to the Vietnam war. I can still hear my Dad's opinion concerning long hair and his forbidding me to let my hair grow. I pledged then and there that I would never mandate hair length for my own children. I smile to think of the irony and of my reaction to my own teenagers who not long ago walked into the house sporting mohawks. I heard my father's voice again. This time it came from within me.

I grew up in a small city where I loved the freedom I had to play baseball with my friends, to ride my bicycle across town, to spend summers at a nearby beach. It was a carefree, fearless time when I was happy, secure and my world was safe. I was the eldest of seven children, but the description does not end there. My Dad had married a woman who found she was unable to conceive, so my brother and I were adopted. I have come to believe that he did not want to adopt. As this was her fervent wish, he agreed for her sake. I can only imagine his reaction when she decided to divorce him and left him with small children. But my father was no stranger to duty. He stepped up to the plate and took care of us and raised us without her. Not long after, he found a second wife, who was a divorcee with three children of her own. Even though my parents were not Lucille Ball and Henry Fonda, we became rather quickly like the film: "Yours, Mine and Ours." This marks what I have reflected upon as being the beginning of our family. They became Dad and Mom to us all and are still today. The "ours" are two more siblings born later. By 1970 our family was complete.

I was able to meet my birth mother and father by the time I was thirty-four. My decision to do so occurred after I started raising my family of eight. I would look at them and see how much they looked like me. I wanted to know not only my family history but also my health history. I had been told very early in life that I was adopted, and I accepted it as a matter of fact. I had parents who cared for me, like all young people around me, and we all accepted each other as a family. Although I have now met my birth parents, who live in different parts of the country with new spouses, and I enjoy a friendly relationship with them and my half sisters, I would never consider them my immediate family. I simply know that the man and woman who raised me are my parents, and the six siblings who were there with me are my brothers and sisters. It all comes back to Dad. He was very, very duty driven. He cared for us even though what happened in his life was not the direct result of his own personal decision. He was not a "jock" of a man. He grew up on a farm. He did not have the opportunity to play a lot of sports other than while he was in the army. I clearly recognize now that he truly sacrificed for our sake. He signed on to coach our Little League team, not because he loved the game as I do to this very day, but because it was an expression of his fatherhood. He wanted his hand on every part of our lives. When I was older and knew the game so much better, I realized some of the directions he gave me were not necessarily correct, or as much by the book as they should have been. But he was my Dad, and that fact is more important than anything else.

My father was a chemical engineer by profession and later moved up in the company directing research and supervising other engineers. He made a run for State Representative one year but lost the primary by a close margin. His intention was to change his profession as he realized that the company was ready to downsize. Early in my last year of high school, the job market changed, and he was no longer needed locally. My eyes were fixed on my hopes for college the following year. He announced to us that the only position opening for him would be in Chicago and that we would have to move there within the month. "Dad," I said, "Please don't make me move in my last year. Besides, I'm going to be accepted at college in this state!" The choice to uproot and move far away is never an easy one, and for my mother, who was a local girl, the prospect of leaving her family would not have been her first choice. "Maybe I could live with Grandma," I pleaded, "and then I'll be in college and away in the fall anyway." I never did ask Grandma about the proposal. Perhaps she or Dad felt that suggestion would not be a good idea. It was a stressful few weeks until my father announced his decision. "I am renting an apartment in Chicago until the spring," he told me. "You will all stay here until then, and I will be home on weekends. If we all left now, the college would designate you as an out of state student, and we would have to pay an exorbitant tuition." I firmly believe my Dad did this for me. Perhaps it was for Mom too, but I was at an age where this decision was critical. I was so happy with my father's solution that no more questions needed to be asked. He was a fair man, although sometimes I thought I received a more rigorous discipline as the elder, physically stronger son. I can only remember once that Dad had a discipline problem with one of us. My half brother, who my father considered rebellious, felt that his step-father had no right to discipline him. He left home for good when he was fifteen, finished high school on his own and has worked here and there ever since. He returned home to be a caregiver for my parents in their old age. It seemed to be a good match, and what they both needed at the time.

I am the proud father of five sons and three daughters. Perhaps that number is unusual for the age, but I am used to a large family! When I noticed my sons could not find a baseball team, I brought some fathers together and we formed our own team. I became the manager, and we enjoyed two years of bonding until my own job called me to make an important decision, much like my father had done. Although I now drive an hour each way to work, my family will stay stable. My children will not have the fear of being uprooted. I still take the boys to watch our own city team, and I still coach them as we watch some of the finer plays. "Watch that catcher," I instructed my son, "see how he slides his catch in quick so the umpire thinks it is a strike?" As I discovered at my son's next game, he had listened and learned. As catcher, he successfully attempted the same tactic!

My oldest son had his uncle's spirit of rebellion in his teenage years. We chose to school him at home so that he would have our special attention. He ran away from home repeatedly in later years and we assisted him by registering him at a halfway house program. When he completed the program, I gave him an ultimatum to come home and accept the house rules or another home would have to be found. It was a toothless threat, but he did decide to return. Living at home was never comfortable for him, but he did graduate from high school and then found a job cooking at a restaurant. For the first time he was able to live away from home. He more recently has chosen to live with his girlfriend. Although he is keenly aware that I do not approve, he has decided for himself as an adult what he wants to do. I do not know what the future will bring for him, but his life is more stable today than in his teenage years. And I am grateful for that. Could it be that he and I might have a similar relationship like my father had with his step-son?

My father has been a constant and steady model for my life. I, too, chose to become an engineer. I have taken on his sense of duty, and I feel it strongly when I relate to my sons. Like my father, I wanted a stable life for my family, so I have made the appropriate sacrifices. My sons must face the additional challenges of a society that presents them with the possibility of disaster from drugs, sex and selfishness. It is a harder time to raise a family. Direction and duty are required more than ever. I recognize the need for constant vigilance to protect them. Like my father, I will be close to seventy when my last child graduates from college. I do not intend to let that prevent me from being a father who knows my duty and nurtures sons who also share the values my father taught me.

If I were to complete my family story, perhaps, my oldest son will be the one who returns to look after my wife and me in our declining years. It could be the eventual vocation of the descendants of Boomers. When that day finally arrives, I welcome the chance to run away from home a few times myself!

## *Learning the Work Ethic*

*Boomers learned from fathers who were often clearly focused on supporting their families and assuring that they would be safe against the possibility of yet another Depression. The example of a strong work ethic was obvious in the home and has certainly had its effects on Boomer children.*

I always considered my family a little different than the neighboring families around us. I was one of ten siblings, a large number even in those days. When I was an infant, my parents moved us to a small agricultural community of 2,500 people. My father was an insurance salesman who was ready to move from place to place as the business demanded. One position brought him to a fine town for raising a family. I remember the summer days where I would be able to pack a lunch and go off for an adventure that would include baseball games, fishing and joining other children of the area for extended playtime. Those were the "Mayberry" days, a peaceful place where we knew our neighbors and they knew us. Parents had a common bond in parenting, and they took up responsibility to watch over any child who came into their purview because they knew that other parents would do the same.

By the time I was in the fifth grade, my father was promoted and moved us to a city of 30,000, thirty miles away. Up to that time I had been in a school that had two classes per grade, but my new school had three classes for each grade! It was a bit of a culture shock for me, and a large adjustment to make at my age. I soon discovered there were benefits to being a part of a larger community. There were opportunities for sports, extra-curricular activities and more possibilities of employment from employers who were looking for teenagers. All of us eventually had a job of some sort. This instilled the work ethic in me and the need to be responsible in learning to manage money. I recall one year my brothers and I had five paper routes, weekly lawn work in the neighborhood, positions in various shops and stores and our own chores at home. My younger sister took on the role as second mother to the younger family members. This freed my older brothers and me to work outside the home on a more regular basis. My father encouraged us in our enthusiasm, and he often told us, "My goal is to work with the insurance salesmen to assure that they will succeed. I'm proud to see you working at such a young age and being successful too!" Dad's support was an important part of that, and we, too, were proud to be out in the workforce, earning our spending money and contributing to the overall success of our family.

My father worked at the office every weekday and came home in time for dinner at 5:00 PM sharp. His family gathered around the massive table for our family time. After dinner, he returned to work for a few more hours for sales calls. "You have to be at their door after they get home," he used to tell us. "A phone call does not make the grade."

Dad was an avid sportsman who had excelled in baseball in his earlier years. He wanted us to participate and expand our abilities. His sons all played baseball, football and other sports. These activities were often our family pastimes as well. We had a large home with a very large yard suitable for sports and other games. I do not remember any period of time that it was not in use. Weekends were always busy, and my father was a central figure in the family barbecues. Our many relatives would visit, and Dad would cook hamburgers and hot dogs, practical fare for such a large number of family and guests. I do not remember having a steak in all the years of my youth. When I found a job at a meat store, I was completely ignorant of the higher grades of meat. I needed to study from a library book so that I would understand the parts of a cow and the names of each cut. It was in those days that I vowed, "When I grow up I will never again eat a casserole." My mother had no choice but to cook institutional size meals that had to be nourishing as well as simple to prepare. From time to time, my father would cook eggs and bacon for breakfast on the weekends, but this was the exception to the rule. My morning meal was usually a large bowl of cereal, after which I was on my way.

Growing up with my father taught me to be responsible, not afraid to try different things and to have a good work ethic. I believe I take my business very seriously today because I watched my father. His goals were to keep a roof over the heads of his large family, and to feed and to clothe us. He did that successfully. If there was anything left over, it was spent on family activities. We did not experience much of the outside world. It was not until the Kennedy assassination that I began to have more access to multiple television stations. Popular music was a means of communication and an enjoyment that could be shared with my friends. Once I had a job, I was also able to discuss the world situation with others in the workplace.

As there were ten children competing for the attention of my father, it was not possible for him to give us all the attention we seemed to demand. A real treat would be anytime he would take just a few of us to a ball game or a special outing. On these outings, we were able to receive more of his attention.

I was married when I was 25 years old. My wife had a three year old son, and I became an instant father. I had no concerns in raising my new son. There was always a little one around the house in my life so this fact seemed very natural to me. I adopted him when he was five; and although he has met his birth father, I have been the only father whom he has known. My wife and I had a strong relationship, and our parents supported the decision to adopt. This son certainly did not have to compete for my time, and I was able to encourage him in my favorite pastime of golf. I remember cutting down an old set of clubs so that his height would not be a detriment to his playing as a youngster. “They’re my size,” he said with delight, “now we can play together!” And play he did, with me and without me. He went on to support high school state championship teams and received a golf scholarship to college. “I’d never thought I’d get tired of golf at school,” he once told me on a trip home, “but it is finally nice to just play for fun!”

I did not fully appreciate what my father had accomplished until I was much older. I would reflect on how he had raised ten children under more difficult financial restrictions and say, “I never could have done that!” He believed that money was not the important emphasis in family life. He wanted to see all his children healthy, fed and making the most out of what they had been given. He did not have the means to pay our college tuition, but he did not put anything into his own pocket either. Today, I see around me so many who only have their own careers in mind. They are the “me generation” that is so foreign to me in my experience of fatherhood.

My father was ecstatic to see how his children had developed. He boasted about his five teachers, an attorney and his business owners. All are married; all but two live in the state, and they provided him the opportunity to be a grandfather twenty three times. Six more have begun another generation. He told his grandchildren what he often told us, “Get a job and stay out of jail!”

My goal for my son was to make sure he received a good education with that business administration edge. He earned his M.B.A., and he is responsible for 700 employees in a large company. I tease him, “You know, you make more money and get more vacations than your father. What’s that about?” I could not be happier for him! My wife and I always shared the responsibility as we taught him life's lessons. We afforded our son more opportunities than either of us were able to have in our earlier years but less than some of his peers enjoy. We did not think it was appropriate to give permission when at sixteen he asked us to approve a spring break trip to Florida. Instead, we offered an alternative we felt was fair and fit with our values. He could go to Florida with a friend, but only if we went along as well.

I would like to think that my son's work ethic was assisted by my example and encouragement. He also learned from my father as they had been good friends throughout the years. Dad died at eighty-four, and was a happy man in his later years. He was surrounded by his family at our many gatherings. Our work never stopped us from honoring the man who instilled the true work ethic in us. My son regularly called my father, and they were often on a golf course together. When were all together, no one could shout "Hey, Dad!" without everyone turning around. I had to refer to my father by his first name in general conversation to avoid confusion as we all had become hard working fathers in our own right. It was a good problem to have! I attribute much of my success to the skills I learned from a man who, with so few resources at the time, achieved so much for his family.

## *Passing on the Torch*

*A father wishes to pass on the values he has come to believe as critical for a happy life. It may be difficult to convince a son of age-old wisdom. Sometimes it requires a good amount of patience. A father waits for that wisdom to prove itself beneficial as his son faces many distractions.*

My father was in the Air Force and his career took him to Biloxi, Mississippi before he was posted to Japan in 1955. I remember the early years of my life being spent on Air Force bases. My younger brother was born on Okinawa and my younger sister in Tokyo. I do not have a clear picture of Japan in my mind, but I do remember we had a Japanese maid and that she taught us a nursery rhyme. That little tune seemed to be a popular one, and many of the military children of the time tell me that they also recall reciting the words.

My mother was a pharmacologist. Her reading and studying helped her to understand the health issues of the day. One article led her to decide to breast feed all her children, which was uncommon for a middle class woman to do at the time. Many mothers chose the purchased formula as their option.

My father grew up in a small farming village in Pennsylvania. He liked the idea of farming, and his attachment to it was obvious as he had a fine garden wherever we lived. In 1959 we returned to the United States, and it was not long before there were two more siblings. Dad purchased a house on the edge of town with a four and a half acre orchard. Nearby there was a flowing stream, and the property was a happy play place for his children. With his degree in business administration, my father was able to find work nearby, and his job no longer meant us being uprooted on a regular basis. Both he and my mother harvested the produce from the orchard and canned the fruit. I remember them both as being a devout couple, but it was Dad who was the religious leader of the family. They were extremely intelligent, and that intelligence was strength for their bond and never a threat to their union.

The earliest memory I have of my father was on our return voyage from Japan. I remember standing on the rail of the ship watching the sunset as he held me. There was no fear of the water below, only the feeling of protection as we stood there together. Neither of my parents acted in such a way as to instill fear in me. I remember one day a neighbor came rushing in to my mother's kitchen in a fright saying, "Your son has climbed to the top of my tree. It's not safe, he is going to fall!" My mother's reaction was, "Oh, that's all right. He's used to climbing trees." The neighbor was horrified that she was not alarmed. Yet, Mom and Dad let us play like boys. Dad often said, "Boys will be boys!" He dismissed it like that. My impression is that some parents were over-protective of their children.

My father was keen to have us not waste any food we had been given. That must have been his depression experience, and I have developed a more "waste not, want not" policy than many of my peers. Earlier, I had thought that everyone was thrifty like me, but many in my own generation have either never had those spendthrift parents, or they have chosen to reject their wisdom. My family cannot understand why I will not replace the ancient lawnmower. My response is "it works just fine. Why replace it when it is not broken?" They walk away shaking their heads because I "just don't get it!" Even my own brother used to have arguments with our father over eating food that he did not like. "Eat what is put in front of you," Dad would tell him, as my brother would turn up his nose at Brussels sprouts or some other vegetable that he would call "exotic and tasteless." My brother later told me that he was grateful for this conflict when he experienced the habits of his friends in the college cafeteria. "They eat only what they like," he told me. "Thanks to Dad I also eat what is good for me!" Today he operates a farm in Wisconsin; he is well-known as a gourmet cook, and yes, he still eats everything!

My father was also an up to date and forward-thinking man. He was involved at his workplace in implementing the emerging computer technology of the 1960s, long before household computers were to become available. I remember looking forward to his occasional business trips as I knew he would purchase gifts for us, souvenirs of his travels. When he was home on weekends, he would play soccer with us in our large yard, using the trees as goal posts. One day a passing stranger stopped to join our game, and my father invited him in for dinner. That was not unlike him, and we often could expect a co-worker or friend to appear at the door near the dinner hour to join us. After the meal he would regularly read to us from the Bible and then give us a blessing before we went out to play or finished our homework. It became a custom and tradition that was special to us. Once, when my father was away, my mother tried to fill in, but as much as I loved her, it seemed different to me than our father's blessing. This was to be his special role alone. This action shaped my idea of fatherhood. He was fair and sometimes strict, treating his children in an equal manner but always there with a blessing. Sometimes I think that the younger siblings had it easier when my father mellowed, but I realize that my parents were regularly in agreement in how their children were to be nurtured and disciplined. I never remember receiving a punishment for anything I did not deserve. Like my father's surprise outings, life was an enjoyable adventure, and I was along for the ride! Perhaps that is why I feel the positive side of the ups and downs of my life. In a recent time of unemployment, I never doubted that things would work out. I recall my father holding me on that ship's rail. Looking down at water that could be dangerous, I could fear that danger or choose to feel secure in my father's arms.

Dad sometimes would bring common sense and humor into his discipline. My younger brother was involved in some mischief with a friend, placing gum in the door locks of some neighborhood homes. He was recognized lingering in the area, and the police were called. My father's reaction was, "Why didn't you run?" He had added insult to my brother's injury. Some people do not appreciate that kind of humor, but I saw him as a man who could say good things about something he did not necessarily like.

His quip, "The best thing about that speaker was how he got to the end and stopped talking!" was his way of lightening up an uncomfortable situation.

My son has come to the conclusion that there is no God, and he is free to pursue the path he chooses in life. His conclusion challenges my whole belief system, but the family has come to avoid any conflict about it. He has developed the unique and entertaining skill of juggling. We encourage him in that, especially as it makes so many happy to see him perform. As he still lives with us after twenty years, perhaps there is yet more time to let our commitment to faith rub off onto him. Our parenting and his maturing are still in progress!

My father lives today on the same property where I grew up, where he had invited some of his grandchildren, including my son, to spend the summer living with him as they worked on area farms. That experience had always gone well, and I know my father's ethics and good judgment was also of benefit to my son. I have some confidence that he will eventually choose the familiar option, the good example of his family, in following his direction in life. I believe in the examples I was taught, I tried to offer those values to my son. Now with a little patience, I will allow him to choose to live his own life.

Many parents around me have said that they do not care what their children do, as long as they are successful. I do not think that this attitude is of benefit to a growing son. I was a teenager in the 1960s and realized that, as Stephen Ambrose said, my father was part of and participant in "The Greatest Generation." I often wonder why these warriors, who stood up to Hitler, did not respond to their children's protests of the 1960s: "Go back to class. You are here to learn, not protest the war! This university is not here to direct foreign policy." Perhaps we would like to look on ourselves as some kind of neutral Switzerland, a peaceful land of strong currency and precision timepieces. I am called a cynic for seeing that our country has become a non-peaceful land of weak currency and cuckoos!

I continue to support my son as he attends college and works on a college research project. My childhood was idyllic by comparison. In my opinion, the education system of my parents was of a higher caliber than what we had in my day. My son's education system has, it seems, deteriorated even further. There may have been acceptance of John Dewey's proposal that rote learning was inappropriate, and that play is the vocation of the young mind. It takes a strong father figure to counteract the trends of selfishness and success at all costs.

I think about that as I now enjoy my eight grandchildren! My father was a strong example of solid values. Inasmuch as I have inherited that torch, I will continue to carry it for my son, and I hope that he will soon accept it from me to carry it onward.

# LATE BOOMERS 1959-1964

Late Boomers bring a new perspective to the study of the era as they have no real experience or memory of the 1950s and grew amid the turbulence of the 1960s. They were children in the 1960s, knowing change as a way of life. They often see something new invented and brought into the home. They are constantly confronted by an ever-growing media that competes for their attention as well as that of their parents.

They are exposed at a very young age to the "feel good" philosophy, the availability of drugs, the moves to the suburbs, the protests and distrust of authority and the trauma of race riots. They are barely teenagers when a President is forced to resign and the Vietnam war is lost. They see the rise of feminism, the beginnings of mothers entering the workforce in large numbers, and their fathers doing more tasks in the home, once the sole responsibility of their mothers. They learn of the early concerns over healthcare and the growth of the environmental movement. The voices they heard spoke of a more secular philosophy that no longer had such a strong emphasis on religion and faith as a methodology for decision making.

Yet, they still come from a home that is strong in post-war roots and they often have siblings with whom to share a common experience. They have the same parents who experienced that war and who nurtured them with similar values and who were seen as role models. Their family experience of the age became their own experience.

The advances they now have experienced will be theirs to accept or to reject. As Late Boomers they are on the leading edge as the age moves forward. They share much in common with Generation X, who will shortly follow them, and they can relate to the Generation X experience. As the last of the Boomers to grow up without the technology that will be so much a part of the lives of those who follow, they form a bridge between generations. They begin to enthusiastically participate in all that the new technology can offer.

## *Fatherhood Across Generations*

*There may be some frustration when a son realizes his children cannot be raised with the same parenting skills that he had experienced. He is led to find new methods to reach the goal of successful fatherhood.*

Boomers like me are going to be part of an enormous segment of the population that will retire and be drawing on what will become the income of our children. They will be the ones to provide for us in the years we will have remaining. I have come to realize that our children will have to support us as much as or even more than we have supported them. Perhaps such expectation of the elderly had been true even before the nuclear family became the norm. For good or for bad, I see my generation being a tremendous financial burden on the country. In the past, a war or two would level all this concern as so many would die. Although we may be living in the shadow of wars and nuclear showdowns and even perhaps nuclear terrorism, I wonder more than worry about the direction in which we seem to be heading.

I grew up in a very large family, experiencing schools with classrooms that were large and could not provide a fewer student to teacher ratio. As I began to enter the workplace, the competition for jobs made me much more competitive. I needed to sharpen my skills in providing a living. The concern for my future was something far off, and the dire prediction for retirement assistance only later came to the forefront as I realized how much the population had grown and how much longer people were living. In more recent years, I have had to think seriously of creating a support system outside of government pensions I once hoped would more greatly assure my well being in retirement.

These concerns have constantly increased as the time has passed. Large families, with the prospected larger numbers to support us, never materialized. Classrooms that once held thirty six students now have decreased to twenty four. My family of four children, which some today would consider large, would have been "a small family" in my youth. Add to that the economy, high consumer prices and the technology opportunities at such a high cost, and we have a recipe for stress any father would recognize.

My father was the epitome of structure and discipline. How else could he organize a home with my siblings and I? When Dad said he was leaving in five minutes, he meant it. There was no question that you would be left behind if you tarried. I remember my disappointment as I watched my brothers and sisters driving off to a shopping trip while I stood in the driveway alone. At four years old that is a hard lesson which I remember to this day. I have become a man who is known for being on time. My children, on the other hand, expect to "finish this game" or reply "I'll be there in a minute," and that behavior is now tolerated by me.

My father was a man of swift and immediate discipline. There was no "counting to ten" or telling you twice. If your elbows were on the table when you were told that was not to be done, there would be a smack. Follow the rules or suffer the consequences. It seems that those choices are gone forever. Some would say that perhaps it is a better thing, that it was brutal, and that parents who would smack their children should be punished themselves. In the disciplining of children, this has brought about a dichotomy in different generations. I have become a "nudger" rather than a smacker and I see my sons responding better to conversation than to a fear of a reaction. However, despite my own father's response to my behavior, I never felt unloved.

I remember my fifth grade science project and how I struggled to complete it. Although he probably could not have cared less about such a project, he appeared from nowhere to assist me without having to be asked. When he saw you were in need of his help, nothing had to be said. For me, that was memorable. He was the same with my brothers and sisters. He had a sense of knowing when we really needed help. That is who I hope to be for my sons, wise enough to know the moment when I am needed as a father. My youngest son has developed a way of letting me know that time has come for intervention. He comes into the room where I am, and sitting down, begins these agitated wiggling motions that let me know his state of stress. I do not sense it is contrived; rather it seems to be a natural thing for him to do in those anxious moments when he has run out of his own ideas and is in need of a father's guidance.

I remember the time that I thought I never needed anything more than those green Converse tennis shoes. Many of my friends had them, and they were a must if you were going to be part of the team at school. There was no way that my parents could afford them at the time, and I figured that my father would say: "Those shoes you have are good enough." Yet, that is not what happened. When Dad found out that I could not be part of the team without them, he made the sacrifice. The shoes arrived the next day. Although I only realized later the sacrifice he had made, it was such a powerful sign of my father's support. Perhaps it has helped me to understand not only my needs, but those of my sons.

My own father was far from the hugging, expressive parent. Like many fathers I hear about he was not known to say "I love you." The time he finally did say it has always had a special place in my memories. My brother and I were not working well together on a project. Dad brought the dissention to a close as he brought us together saying, "You two are just like me in many ways. I love you more than I can tell you. Now, I want you to get along!" I can remember we repaired the rift that very day.

I didn't always listen to my father's advice, however. When I was eighteen and knew what was best for me, I told my parents that I was going to get married. Expectedly, Dad said I was too young. But who was I to listen? As can be expected, my decision came back to haunt me, as often happens to those who refuse to listen. To make a long story short, the marriage was childless and over in five years. Dad never said "I told you so!" He was not one to condemn or chastise. Perhaps he knew that I had learned from this and did not need recrimination in a time of healing. The second time around I took more time and that has proven to be the key. What is even more encouraging is that my father has always supported me, and the four children from my marriage are special to him.

When my oldest son reached eighteen he remained in the home and told me that as he had reached an age where he could make his own decisions on attending the things we did as a family. I miss the daily family meals that were a part of my growing up. They were such a great time of communication and support for all our activities. Even though schedules make daily family meals impossible, I continue to encourage the family to be together for mealtimes. I had to express to my eighteen year old about the rules under our roof. I worried that in enforcing this discipline I could alienated him from me or from the ethics I wished to encourage. That we spend time together as a family is an important discipline for us. While he was there begrudgingly, I struggled with the worry that my insistence would distance him from the family. I believe that family will be a source of strength for him throughout his life. Time will tell, but I stuck to my guns on that one. My parents had a policy that once you left home, you did not move back in. It was their way of treating all their children with fairness. As their youngest son,

I was not exempt from the rule. Even though for many years my grandmother lived in a "Granny apartment' attached to my parent's house, it was time after all those years for my parents to be in a nest without their children. It does not seem to be a Boomer age custom for Boomers to have their parents living with them. This must have been a great sacrifice as it was more common in the last generation. Even though our parents are living longer today, they do not seem to be living in their children's homes in their later years.

My Dad was a jack-of-all-trades. He taught us to be self-sufficient. As I saw him lying on his death bed, I reflected on how much stronger a father I was because of him. As I stood there with my brother, and remembered how long ago Dad encouraged us to get along, we said a prayer together, the three of us. It reinforced in my mind the image I have of God as a father. It will continue as a noble aspiration for me as I hope it will also be for my son.

## *Fatherhood That Nurtures Family*

*Fathers in our society do not find expressions of love come easily. When a father is able to express that love verbally, his family often grows strong and secure. When a son hears those words from his father at any age, he is changed for a lifetime.*

Perhaps older Boomers were affected more by the influences of proximity to the World War II years, nonetheless I have so much more in common with them than the succeeding generation. Some of those characteristics include the concern over healthcare and its costs, the "earthly" environmental and ecology movements, more personal freedoms than ever before, and the tendency to be a self-absorbed "me" generation. I have come to realize that many Boomers say "me first!" and I contrast that to the experience of my father, whose prime focus always seemed to be the family. My generation has changed the way families are raised. I have noticed a more self-indulgent era where daycare is common as parents work longer and harder to provide the conveniences and contrivances of the modern world, sacrificing many of the values that nourished me and which I believe to be critical in raising a family. Perhaps I have fallen victim to some of what I see as those negative influences, but when I think of Dad, I consider him as lucky to have avoided what many fathers face today. It makes me sad to watch the egocentric emphasis growing even greater, spiraling society and the family downward.

When I was a teenager, my goals in life were to be a success in business, to have a good job, a comfortable house, to marry and to raise a happy family. I never sought fame or a name for myself, and I look back on those as reasonable and healthy goals. Now in my forties, I am happy to say that I was able to meet all my teenage ambitions for my life. Today my reflections concern how I will re-invent myself, establishing new goals upon which I can reflect, adjust and be more relaxed as I work toward their implementation. I have no intention of worrying, at this late date, as to whether I can meet these new goals for the rest of my life.

This has been the first year of the "empty nest" experience for my wife and me. I now have time to ponder what will be my new level of involvement in the lives of my children will be. My goals in raising a family and providing for them have been met, and I have been able to assist my children to finish college. I have seen one child enter a happy marriage and now look forward to becoming a "Grandboomer!" Perhaps satisfaction comes from having set for myself realistic goals that I could accomplish using my abilities, knowing my limitations and while dedicating myself to my family first. To me, being a good father means the relationship I have with my children is far more important than the relationship I have with my job. I remember being laid off early in my career and feeling very vulnerable in the face of my responsibility to provide. I believe that faith helped me in that struggle. As I was faced with house payments, growing children and so many things dependent on my salary, I needed more than the power of my own resolve. My trust in God, my faith and my prayers were the power that made the difference until that secure job came my way. I hope my children will have their faith to help them when life gets difficult.

My father was a purposeful, committed farming man of German descent who exposed us to occasional fits of temper, but he let us know his feelings on discipline and behavior. I was in a favorable position of being the youngest of six siblings, able to watch how Dad related and disciplined the older children. I was wise enough to try to avoid repeating their mistakes. There were times I was spanked, as was the custom of our age, but I never had any doubt that this discipline was done with concern and love and not anger.

After a well-deserved punishment, I recall repeating to myself,"I know he loves me! I know he loves me!" Like so many fathers I heard about in my day, and stereotypical of German fathers, my father had a problem with the words "I love you." I remember telling him how I felt about that when I was only fourteen. Raised on a farm, I was driving tractors and vehicles at a very early age. It was not unknown to drive the car short distances around the farm without a license. Once I was speeding on a gravel road I swerved and hit a tree. Although I was not hurt, there was serious damage to the car. Not unexpectedly, my father was very upset. He trusted me to be careful, and I let him down. Amid his angry tirade over my carelessness, I blurted out, "You always are yelling at me but you never tell me that you love me." It seems I needed to hear the words spoken, though I should never have doubted his love for me. So many times he showed pride in us when he took us hunting and fishing. Even my mother joined in and had become quite the expert herself! All the vacations were about us, spending time with us, showing us the things he had learned about survival. Ultimately, he taught us firsthand about the happiness that comes from sharing and nurturing a family. My father was a frugal man who accomplished all of this without excess or luxury.

Once, on a hunting trip with Dad, I was able to ask him about his life and his time growing up. He told me that his lack of education did not stop him from having a successful farming career, but he wanted me to know that similar paths to success were not much less common today. Finishing my education was critical if I was to be a success. I remember him saying that he would do all he could to help me, just as he had helped all his children. There was security in knowing that this was his way of saying how much he loved me. These trips were an opportunity for him to talk about his relationship with his own father and why hunting was such an important a part of his life. My grandfather owned the land where we would hunt and would often join us on those days.

On one such an occasion, we were all out hunting and my grandfather decided to go off to his favorite site while Dad and I stayed together. It was only a few months after my sixteenth birthday, and I was hoping to shoot my first buck. As a prime specimen came out of the distant bush, my hopes were fulfilled as I aimed, fired off a single shot and watched the deer fall. Dad smiled at my first success, and I felt a special bonding with him. An hour later Dad enjoyed a similar success of his own.

My grandfather would later succumb to a heart attack on one of his hunting trips. Dad and I found him on his property late one day, when he had not returned as expected. I remember my father saying, "Well, it is how he would have wanted to go."

I want my son to realize that I will die a happy man knowing that I have always been concerned for his interests. I have coached him in sports, watched him finally begin to listen and take seriously the bits of advice I have offered from time to time. I trust he knows how much I love him. I hope he will be strong when I am no longer there. I think of when my own father was dying, I questioned if I had been a good son to him. I told him, "I hope that I have given you as much joy as my sons have given me." He looked at me, responding with an earnest, "Most certainly!" I wanted to know that I had made him proud and was the son he wanted me to be. I was lucky enough to be able to tell my Dad how well he had measured up as a father. Even though he only lived to be sixty three, his life had been rich. His sons had grown to be fine men and fathers. He died on July fourth, and I remember the fireworks and the family celebrations around us, and how that year we could not share in the joy of them. Even so, the world went on around us, and I reflected how we would eventually move on as well. It taught me to live more in the day, for example, not to wait until that twenty-fifth anniversary for that celebratory trip which we always had hoped to take. As a Boomer, I have become more caught up in today than saving for tomorrow. How could I not say yes to helping my son when he was accepted to Harvard? We trusted in God and with enthusiasm found the loans and grants and scholarships! My support can only encourage my sons not to put up boundaries and barriers in their lives that come from fear of failing. With a family, you cannot fail! I would remind them of my attitude in making that decision: "It's Harvard, and how can we not afford it?"

As I grow older, I intend to give even more time to my son. Even though geography has increasingly become more a problem to families trying to maintain close ties, I really want to see his family, to see him mature as a parent. I smile to think of the lessons he will learn repeating the same disciplines he vowed he would never repeat as a parent! I encourage him not to be overcome with the worry about 'provisions.' I remind him of that morning in the car when he asked, "How come everyone else has a satellite dish but us?" It was an interesting learning curve that taught him "what does not kill you will make you stronger!" As Dad used to say: "When you experience a hard winter, you appreciate the spring all the more." I sit back in the family room with my son to watch today's game, and I look at the spring and all that blooms to life outside. This moment reminds me of all the games Dad and I watched together and how much I respected and emulated my father. I want to believe that my son feels the same way about me.

## *Fatherhood in the Formative Years*

*The attention that fathers give to their sons is often interrupted by the necessity of working for the family's material welfare. Often there is not a second chance to make up for lost years and lost time.*

I was my Dad's only son. My two sisters and I grew up in this age of technology and population boom. In that sense, we certainly were "Boomers." There were many improvements around us, many opportunities made possible to us that my father would never have dreamed of when he was growing up. He taught me in a most positive way about securing my family lovingly, as well as financially. Even though I live today in an age of easily accessible information and other societal advances, there are also inherent issues this age has brought about that are not so good. As a Baby Boomer parent, I often reflect upon the rushed pace of family life, the busyness and the stress. These aspects are all unhealthy and not the lifestyle I want for my sons. I want them to remember a happy, supportive family life where they were safe and felt secure in their surroundings. I yearn for a life uncontrolled by outside influences that draw me away from my family and all that necessary quality time I wish to give them. In my heart I know that this time would be more important than what I could provide them as a result of a maximum work load, but in my head I still find myself caught in the race to improve status and to increase wealth.

In earlier days, the summer brought weekends at the lake where Dad would shower all his attention on us. He seemed always to be involved in what we were doing, sharing with us true quality time. I can count twelve years where my sisters and I delighted in our family life nurtured by Dad and Mom.

This taught me about the meaning of family as well as the true value of life.

My father would talk to me about his father and what he had taught Dad concerning parenting and success. Even though he had died many years before, his words came alive in how my father taught us by example. He believed in finishing what you start. Do not move onto the next project until this one is finished. I remember how he put that idea into practice at a time when my whole life revolved around a bright red snowmobile that I was going to restore. The process had taken many years and as I grew older my mind wandered to the idea of buying a car. Since I was sixteen years old, Dad felt I had a few things to learn about being focused on one thing at a time. My father let me sell it and purchase my first car only when I completed the renovation work on the snowmobile.

There was a similar experience ahead for me when I made the high school basketball team. A few weeks after I began, I decided to quit. "Keep working at it," Dad assured me. "It is way too soon to give up!" Sure enough, he was right. By the ninth game, I not only excelled, but became a starter. In my junior and senior years, I became team captain. I shudder at the thought that on my own I never would have experienced this success. There were many more which followed!

I also learned my skills of parenting from Dad. He knew that the word "no" had to be used with care. So many parents seem afraid to use that word now. Perhaps parents feel that no means a denial of love. Perhaps some believe that nothing should be denied to anyone. I believe that when you create a false impression for children about life and call that love, you make a huge mistake.

There is no such thing as blind luck in life situations. Luck is where preparation meets opportunity. In my business life, my father taught me a sound work ethic, organization, discipline and perseverance. With these you will be successful. This approach works for my home as well, where I practice the same discipline and structure. My wife and I work as a team and although things are not always easy, I believe that our endeavor has been a success. This success did not come about overnight. Some years ago, it took me some time to realize and change an unhealthy pace to my life, one which was causing stress on my family. Perhaps it was my Dad who was the first to notice it. With his usual gentle smile he said to me one day, "Your whole family looks tired. What have you been up to?" Those words caused me to pause and think. I thought I was the only one who was tired. That night things began to change. Dad had experienced a complete change in his business and in his future when his company was victim to a hostile takeover. The way he coped with that, and the way he kept us secure through that experience, was an inspiration to me. Even though this must have been a time of terrible stress for my father, he did not allow that stress to change the peace of our family life.

We began our family early and thought we had completed our years of having more children when we were given a second chance at being parents. This time I was determined to protect my new son from the stress and problems of a young, inexperienced family. My older children wanted to be actively involved in his care. From my son's birth at the hospital to the many feeding times, we put in a collective effort for this new family member. The time went by fast for the older children. I am now in my forties and I am enjoying every stage of this new growth. My wife and I are slowing this family down. The delivery room was an incredible bonding time for us all. My daughters burst into tears at the sight of their new brother. My son has become a galvanizing experience for my whole family. As I see my children respond to and love their new brother, I come to realize the beginning of a more giving family. They may have once enjoyed our fast pace, our active social schedule, but the family did suffer in the process.

My younger son will have a different experience of life than his siblings. He is likely to be living alone with my wife and me during his teenage years. I know I will have even more time for him as he will eventually be the only child at home. He will also be blessed with something many children do not have these days: a stay-at-home Mom. I cannot overstate how important her decision has been to me and the children. The security she brings to family is worth more than all the money she could have made. I am so happy she made this choice at a time that many women choose not to do so. I also was fortunate enough to have a stay at home Mom. Another thing that the fast paced family life has led to is fast paced parenting, or even worse, no parenting at all.

I have often thought that our family is descended from a long line of love and support. I see that in the occasions when we celebrate as one large family. A few years ago, the highlight of our family gatherings that year was the fiftieth anniversary of Mom and Dad's marriage. As we gathered at the altar surrounding them and they renewed their vows, I knew that anything I achieved was closely connected to their love and that this love was for us all and for our children. My ultimate responsibility is to see that this love continues. As I held my young son that day, I felt warm in the knowledge that their love was real and lasting. I was, after all, my father's son. The greatest tribute I can give him is to be with my son and, like Dad, to keep that relationship strong.

## *Fatherhood & Sibling Death*

*The security and peace of a family is deeply affected by the death of a son. The words and actions of a father at this time will make the difference between healthy growth and long lasting, negative effects.*

My life as a Boomer has been shaped and defined by a single phone call that came to our home in my early teenage years. An operator from Boston put through a call, making sure that my father was on the line before an official voice told us that my oldest brother, sixteen years my senior, had been killed in a horrific car accident. Here ended what I considered happier, carefree times and began the pall of grief that settled over my family. That event still has influence over my siblings to this day.

In general, I really am unaware how I have been affected by the Boomer age itself. Perhaps I have noticed a man's role expanding in the home. Work that was before the task of the wife, such as changing diapers, cooking, household chores, is now more and more commonly shared by father and mother. There has been a breaking down of stereotypes, but at the same time an emphasis on self-gratification. In my father's age, some desires would be delayed while the Boomers came to expect things immediately as the "right now generation." My Dad used to say, "Today's luxuries will become tomorrow's needs," and he was right. As the youngest of seven children, I understood that I would be benefiting from some of the trickledown effect. My parents had already lost my twin at birth and another child, a baby I never knew. Our ages ranged over sixteen years, most of the span of the Boomer generation. My Dad, like many fathers of Boomers, had served in the Second World War. He tried to enlist at seventeen, but was held up until he reached his eighteenth birthday. Patriotic, but a conscientious objector, he served as a communications installer and was wounded at Saipan. His parents received the word erroneously that he had been killed, grieved their loss like many in those days, and bore it bravely until one day they were surprised when he walked, smiling and very much alive, through the door. He benefited from the G.I. Bill, using the education to become an accountant. His whole life proceeded in such a fashion. He surprised us with his wit, his humor, and then confused us with the mixed message that came from the aspirations of a middle class man. He was a bit of a puzzle at first until I came to better understand him.

With the value of further education firmly in his mind, it was his intention that his children should also find success. His first born son went off to an Ivy League college where he excelled in landscape architecture and became a respected professor very early in life. This first achievement became the model for the rest of us.

Watching my Dad, I came to realize how much he loved all people. He had the same rapport with the custodial staff as he did with the top brass, an ability to relate to the lowest and to the highest. He had such a sense of humor that you did not mind when he told a joke and ruined the punch line or when he laughed at the wrong time. He used to bring me along on his visits to the V.A. hospital, calling me his "trump card." These times ended any phobia I may have developed about hospitals or the sick. Since I was with him so often, being the youngest, I asked him one day," Dad, who is your favorite?" With that twinkle in his eye he took no time to answer, "You are all my favorites, just extremely different favorites!" Yet there were times I would get mixed messages about how he reacted. If I chose the wrong tool from his toolbox, I'd get a good wrap on the knuckles. "Learn those tools," he would growl.

But you could not help but laughing as he was, and still is, such a character! I will not forget the sight of him placing flags on the military members' graves at the end of May, the appreciated relief of a moment of laughter he brought to families when he visited funeral homes, his well-known Marx Brothers routines, or his recurring role as a popular local Santa Claus. That was how I discovered the real Santa. I ran into him and knocked him over as I raced out into the back yard one snowy December night. I never realized until then that Santa knew how to curse in Italian!

As a father, I think that the example of the great love I have for my wife is an important influence on my sons. I believe that I must instill some faith in them so they can better overcome future grief like that my family shared following the death of my oldest brother. While life can seem miserable in the face of such tragedies, I have come to believe that the experience can still be a great blessing. I try to show this to my oldest son today. Even though I was depressed and my parents devastated, when my brother died counseling was not common as it is today. In our case, we were unable to see the body because of the seriousness of the accident. This left an emptiness that only heightened our grief. I do not want any son of mine angry at God as I was! I attempt to show my son the reality of death by inviting him to the funeral home for the death of someone he may know. While I do not force him, I make the invitation and he often accepts it. His reaction has often taken the form of questions about death and expressions of concern for the family. More often his statement will reflect the reality of death. "They're in heaven now," he tells me.

As I live each day in a celebratory way, realizing it could be my last, I tell my son, "I will die too, one day, but you will always have my spirit with you!" He seems to accept that as a hopeful promise. I cannot bear to think of him grieving in the way we did those first few years after the accident, becoming introverted or neglecting to socialize as he goes through the separation process. Dad's unhappy reaction was to lose focus and damage his longstanding relationships. I, on the other hand, went through many jobs until I was able to confront my denial and face the reality that life would go on. Today, I believe I am fortified to react to tragedy in a wholly different and healthy way. I will always be there for my son.

I wish I had been able to spend more time in serious conversation with my father. Perhaps it was not common for fathers and sons to open up to each other in those years. As the provider, my father did not always have the time. My mother served the role of advisor and confidant, and I talked to her for hours about what was in my heart. It was untimely that she died at only sixty-nine years old. Dad's warm smile has lived on into his eighty-seventh year. He is not strong any more, and his memory is fleeting, but he still lives in the family home where we all grew up. His four remaining children watch over him, and I take my turn to make sure he has company day after day. When he is with people, he is a much happier man and the man I will always remember.

My son will grow to be a sensitive, faithful, intelligent man who will have his choice of many careers. He excels in academics, music and athletics. "Look out for that lonely one around you, for that is the person who needs your help," I have told him. I have seen that he does indeed look around now, of his own accord.

On reflection, perhaps I would not want to change anything about my era. I often wish that I had a deeper faith earlier in my life so that I may have been stronger when faced with tragedy. But I have also learned that faith is something that grows as you live. I have come to believe that things will all work out as long as I stop interfering! I've come to believe that the difference between a job and a career is that a career takes an extra ten hours a week of work! My profession as a physiotherapist has taught me on so many occasions that when I give, so much more comes back to me. My family is no exception to that rule. I am glad that I offered my time to my Dad in his last years, and have no regrets now that he has passed away. As I see the family smile appear on the face of my son, I understand deeply the sentiment of Lou Gehrig. I know he would forgive me for paraphrasing him, but like him, I sincerely believe that today "I am the happiest father on the face of this earth!"

## *A Strong Father Figure*

*The importance of strength in the face of adversity and tragedy is a powerful witness for any son. A father wants his own son to benefit from that strength as he begins to face his own life's challenges.*

I'll sum it up for you in three words: "time of change." This Baby Boomer age has certainly been that. Everything in my life has been affected. Very little that I anticipated in my youth has turned out in the way I originally expected. I just don't believe it was like this for my father or grandfather. Certainly things changed for them, but I must admit, the pace of life since the 1960s has been astounding. As I talk to my friends and I hear of their experiences, it seems that my views are correct. Perhaps life has affected us differently with the tremendous changes in technology. I feel I have kept on top of it all to some extent, but as new innovations continue to enter my life, I wonder how much longer it will be before I am left behind. Don't get me wrong. I'm not saying that all this has been a bad thing for me. It has just been stressful as I watch the world evolve around me.

I am a rather late Boomer having been born in 1959. Even though the 1960s seemed to encourage the spirit of change and were my formative years, I still feel more connected to the age of my parents and the discipline of their lives. I view some of the customs of the modern age as disrespectful. I have attempted to instill my values in my sons. I have come to realize that they have not only listened, but they have learned. I am talking about the visual things, like dressing appropriately at special events or at weddings. I believe that your dress shows others you honor them and respect the occasion. Perhaps that person may not even care what I wear, but I want them to know that I think their event is a special one. With my attire and customs that are not just for “every day” I show them I respect and celebrate their special day.

I have always believed in the importance of the family sharing at least one meal a day together. When I was a boy, my father cooked Sunday brunch. It was a special family time. We found the time to be there because it was a sacred moment for us as family. I notice that recent ads on T.V. have picked up on that theme of the importance of the family meal. I am comforted by this return to tradition. I believe a family meal can be key to addressing some serious problems that we have in our homes. Families are being torn apart in our society by conflicting schedules, parents work demands, societal pressures, greed, the troubled economy and the general fear and malaise that have characterized post 9/11 America. People can try to ignore these problems and carry on, but I see that response as a form of denial. These things need to be talked about in a nourishing and protected environment. My Dad was the one who guided the family through its various, and small by comparison, “crises.” He coached the little league with such energy that I pledged I would do the same for my boys. That sort of connectedness has made a difference in my family.

Perhaps ‘connection’ is an important concept, especially for a Boomer. When I was seven, my Dad took me out to the lake on many Saturdays. He reserved a boat; and with poles and lunch in hand, we headed out to our special fishing place and time together. This time was so important that the weather had no effect upon it. I can remember many weekends of rain where I thought he would surely cancel our outing, but that did not happen. He took that time to be with me. I remember how I felt as my young mind realized this was an expression of his love. How can I not pass the same thing on to my boys? I know what a Dad feels like, and I want them to know it as well.

My father showed me the greatest act of love in his reaction to the cancer that developed in my brother. My brother was three years younger than I and I helped him along through life. God must have known our family could handle this trial with grace and love. Our family had developed a built-in trust and a belief structure that supported us, as we supported my brother. He had cancer of the spinal cord. Eventually he was paralyzed from the waist down. Dad directed all the possible attention to him, even taking leave from work. More and more sacrifices would become required of us as the disease progressed. But Dad was determined that we would do it all at home. Mom told me that this was not the first time Dad had experienced cancer. He had lost his mother to the illness when he was eight. She said he had taken it the hardest then but had been the strongest in his family.

I remember one particular Friday night as my Dad had encouraged me to head off to the football game. He said that he would take care of my brother alone that night. It did not seem like that fall evening was out of the ordinary; my brother did not seem any worse, but he was on my mind throughout the game. I did not delay in getting home when the game was over. I could see his bedroom window was dark as my friends dropped me off in front of the house. I thought that was unusual, and even stranger was seeing Mom waiting on the porch. "Your brother and your father have gone to the hospital," she told me. "I wanted to wait for you." "What happened?" I asked. She told me that the doctor was sure it was a brain tumor. We got into the car and headed for the hospital. We were all in the room together for what turned out to be our last goodbye. My brother died in the early hours of the next morning at only fourteen years old. I think that Dad took it the hardest, but again he proved himself to be strong for us.

I believe that I have learned how to discuss things openly in my family. We understand something about death. My sons have learned not only from the stories I told them about Dad and my brother, but also from their own experience when their grandmother died. I was happy to see the relationship that my sons had with her and how they learned to grieve, in their own way, through their personal relationship with my Mom. Today they have a special relationship with their grandfather who has survived into his eighties and continues to be greatly respected in our family.

I am satisfied that my sons are as connected to my era as I was connected to my father's era. Perhaps there has been too much said, too much concern expressed about this generation. A lot of energy has been expended when, as it turns out, this generation been doing pretty well considering all that has challenged them. My times had the stress of the Vietnam war and a loss of confidence in authority figures. My sons have experienced yet another war and more disappointments from those in positions of authority. The lessons I have shared with them, fortified by the strength I received from my Dad, and how my sons have processed their own experiences of fatherhood, will safely bring them through their era. I am confident that they have received the support they will need as they grow into being good men and good fathers.

## *Converting Tragedy*

*A father can teach his son how to respond to the crises and tragedies of life in a healthy and positive manner. Realizing that all people must face hardship at one time or another, a father can show his son how to cope with sadness and move forward with life.*

My parents had come from Tennessee, moving farther north after the war as jobs were more plentiful in the more northern states. I was born on the very day and at the very hour of the Kennedy assassination. I began my life on the day of a national tragedy and would learn, with my father's help, to face my own personal tragedies as well. My mother often told me the story of being rolled into the recovery room and hearing a nurse announce that the President had been shot. It had yet to be confirmed that he had actually been assassinated. I feel that this day is a key marker in the life of Baby Boomers, and I share that in common with them. I grew up being able to tell that story as a small claim to a sort of fame or at least a connection to the era. Another mark of coincidence in my family was the fact that all of us had birthdays and important events that were on or near to the twenty second of the month. For example, my sister was born on December 24, which was forever a source of annoyance to her, as her birthday was so close to Christmas.

My earliest memories surround the horrors of the race riots in 1967. Throughout that summer, we who lived in the center of the city were in constant fear as our world erupted into violence around us. I remember my father having his shotgun close by as gangs roamed the streets around us, terrorizing, looting and burning. Whenever they came near to our house, he would fire a warning shot and scream at them, "I'm not afraid to shoot!" He made sure they saw the barrel of the gun pointed in their direction. These vandals were cowardly thugs who had no respect for authority. The police were overwhelmed with calls, and even with assistance from neighboring officers, they could not be everywhere that danger lurked. Residents were often on their own to fend off attack and injury. So my father nailed our windows down and kept watch, gun in hand, every night of those hot summer months. During the day, his job took him to the suburbs where he worked at a factory producing railway cars. He was our protector, always home with us before nightfall. The crisis subsided after the hot weather diminished, but the National Guard roamed the city for months, assuring that peace was indeed restored. For me, this experience was the most vivid memory of my pre-teen years, and it left a deep impression. It is not far from my thoughts whenever I go into the downtown of any American city today.

When I was eight, my father moved our family out into the suburbs and closer to his workplace. He wanted to avoid the unrest, and the rising racial tension, and put behind him that horrible summer of 1967. In our new location there seemed to be more fresh air and as we grew, there was an availability of jobs for me and my four siblings. By the time I was fourteen I had worked delivering newspapers, and my older brother and I had a job at a local pizzeria. However, my father's hopes of safety and peace were soon to be shattered. One afternoon while I was working at that pizzeria, a day my brother was not on duty with me, the phone rang. My sister was on the line and cried out, "Come home now. Mom needs you." I heard screams and crying in the background. "What happened?" I asked. "He's dead. They've shot him on the way to work!" she sobbed. I rushed in to the manager's office and told him why I had to leave immediately. I just ran and ran until I could see our house. Confusion and panic was ensuing, police cars on the road and in our driveway, and I could hear the sound of an ambulance siren in the distance. It was utter chaos. The police would not let me near the car where I could only presume my brother was lying dead, and I rushed into the house to find my mother sobbing inconsolably. "Where's Dad?" I demanded. My sister told me that he was on his way and that they had also called for my oldest brother, who was a Marine in California. The story was soon related that my brother had been in a confrontation at a nearby corner as his car partially blocked the intersection. Words were exchanged, and a sixteen year old had taken out a 410 gauge shotgun and fired at point blank range. My seventeen year old brother, the person I was closest to in the whole world, was instantly killed. His friend, who was a passenger in the car, witnessed everything, drove my brother those few blocks home, where my mother rushed out of the house and was the first to see her son. It did not take them long to find and arrest the assailant. My first reaction and the reaction of my oldest brother was to seek revenge. Our father sat us down to explain, "Let the law do its work. They have caught him. Remember, he is sixteen years old."

I do not know where he received the strength to react in such a rational way, but as he was my father, I accepted his wisdom. The court case resulted in the youth going to jail for a year and a half, after which he was released. I simply had to accept the fact that the person who killed my brother was on the street again in so short a time for so great a crime. In the years that followed, my parents did not talk about the tragedy. There were no pictures of my brother around the house, but rather a sense of denial of it all. I still feel a little emptiness when he occasionally comes to mind. I took out his photograph one day and showed my son his picture. I wanted him to know that he had another uncle. That was important to me, and I wanted it to be important to him as well. "He looks like Grandma, Dad," he told me. I had forgotten that resemblance, and it was good to hear it recalled.

I did not do well in school after that time, and at sixteen I found a good job pouring concrete. I married at 18, immediately began to raise a family, and I worked for a construction company until a 1989 accident injured my knee and resulted in time off work. During my long recovery period, I had the opportunity to study and complete my high school equivalency, and then later a year of college level courses. That hard work paid off in an even better job for me as I returned to the concrete business.

My father was the one who first taught me the merits of hard work. I remember the time we completely tore down a car engine and rebuilt it. He would say, "The reason this works so well is that all the parts are working together. Take away any one of them, and the whole thing will collapse." I have found that is true in life as well. I feel strongly that a son needs both a father and a mother ensuring that he grows and matures well. We almost lost Dad when he was forty seven. His heart bypass and eventual removal of one of his kidneys took a serious toll on him. I know my Dad would have loved to have spent more time with me, and he did what he could, despite the work restrictions on his time and the health restrictions on his energy level. I believe I compensated for that in the life of my own son by going on our fishing trips, coaching his baseball team and playing catch in the yard whenever we were home together.

I regret that I did not spend more time with my father. I wish that I could turn the clock back, that he had not died of an aneurism in 1997, and that my brother had not been killed. I know that is impossible, but my life would have been completely different.

My father was a loving person who worked hard to support his wife and children. I think he would have done anything to make us happy. He did not live long enough to enjoy all the benefits of the life he had created. I worry a bit that high blood pressure has been prevalent in our family that I might also succumb to it. I try to live in a healthy manner so my son will have me around for at least a few more years! We have developed a strong relationship. I taught him to care for other people and to respect the law. He chose to become a police officer, and I am proud of his choice. I know my father would have also been proud. My wife and I worry about the possible danger in which that choice places him. We refrain from talking about that together. We know that at least his rural position is safer than an urban location. He calls me every week and talks to me for at least thirty minutes. That has eased my apprehensions somewhat. The distance between us has not diminished the affection we both feel for each other. As my Dad always said, "Hard work pays off." It could also be said that fatherhood is hard work. I know in my father's case it certainly has paid off! I have absolutely no reason to believe that it will be different for my son.

## *The Importance of Trust*

*A son is very much aware of the expressions of trust that come from his father. Trust is a special expression of confidence and a son learns to prize that respect and act in such a way that the trust given to him is justified.*

I grew up as what I would call a "free-lance kid." I lived in an urban neighborhood in a block of twenty six houses where there was an average of three children per family. The street was our playground, and we were outside all the time as our parents always encouraged us in making many friendships in the neighborhood. In fact, our home was "play central." Our back yard was so much the center of activity that the grass really never grew, and my mother had to give up what must have been her desire to have a garden or at least some flowers. Our yard became a dirt lot where children's loud voices were common and where a day did not go by that my parents did not feel they were owners of one large playpen. My siblings and I never watched that much television in those years; we were simply too active in our outdoor events. The summertime only increased the hours of our activities, and we grew oblivious to the changing outside world and its cultural problems that would eventually encroach upon our urban lifestyle in the later 1960s.

My father never gave me the feeling they were keeping a tight rein on me, but they did know where we were every minute; and I don't think he ever failed to call for me that I was not in earshot to respond to his request. As a tightly knit smaller community within a larger urban sprawl, I believe the neighborhood parents were comfortable in knowing that their children were nearby and with each other. That reassurance must have brought some security and peace for them. We were a creative group of young people. I remember the years that we put on neighborhood fairs and markets in our yards. This was totally conceived and assembled by the youth themselves. Natural leadership seemed to emerge as children from six to seventeen actively participated in events of their own production. We would organize a demolition derby using old shopping carts where no one was ever hurt. Rarely was there ever a fight among us. I remember in those late Decembers the collection of used Christmas trees that were stacked in our back yard for the creation of forts and play places for the cold winter months. Our parents did not seem to mind the use of our property, and their permission only encouraged our new ideas. I recall the igloos we used to build. I argued with my brothers over being first to wear those necessary woolen mittens so that I could dip my hands into cold water and form the snow and ice into blocks. Each May a chunk of ice in our yard was still there as the trees turned green, and the first weeds made their desperate attempt to take over the ground.

It was an age when at least one of your parents was present in the house at all times and a time when no one had ever heard of daycare. I have a strong feeling today that mothers sell their families short as they leave home to provide the extra income. My father's priority had always been about children. He was a physical education teacher for 33 years. The benefits of having him home on nearly every weekend and all those summer days was obvious to me then as much as today. He had been a navy frogman in the war, and he took special pride in the small pool he constructed each year in our yard where he was careful to enforce rules on how and when it was to be used. I respected those restrictions as a matter of fact from a father whose navy exploits during the war were the stuff of which legends were made. I never gave our meager economic status on his teacher's salary any thought as we were never without the necessities of food, clothing and warmth. I was satisfied even knowing some neighbors had more than I, yet it was our small home that was often the meeting place for them. We were the hangout place because our friends felt welcome. The customs that included walking to school, home for lunch and back to school and home again on a daily basis were common in our neighborhood. We knew our neighbors, and we seemed to share the same value system. The race riots of the 1960s barely touched our area, although the presence of tanks and police protecting our streets is the point in my life where things began to change. The crisis did not last long, however, and our streets returned to normal; our friends continued their traditions. In fact, my father stayed in the home another twenty five years even long after the exodus to the suburbs changed the face of our community.

Dad was never afraid to play rough. I remember his wrestling bouts with my brother, which was for me a time to avoid their playful yet tough competition. This caused me to feel somewhat less athletic, but Dad made up for that by letting me know he saw my strength in my intelligence. He'd say, "Here comes my intelligent one." I have often thought he was wrong about that in that, I never attended college, but he seems to have seen something in me that superseded a formal education. Looking back, I am shocked to remember that he once let me go on a trip with a friend across the country to California when I was only sixteen. This could only have come from trusting that I was mature enough to accomplish what was necessary. The following year when my friend backed out of a trip we had planned to go north, my Dad volunteered, "That's all right, I'll go with you." I was indeed surprised. Not only that, but he let me plan, navigate and drive throughout the entire twelve days. We camped, hiked, had quality time together, and I was proud to show him all those places I had seen before on an earlier class trip. Dad seemed to take it all with awestruck enjoyment. I remember one of the days I obviously was lost and discovered my mistake so I stopped the car to read the map. My Dad, who was asleep in the front seat beside me opened one eye and teased, "Did Magellan make the wrong turn?" And he laughed and, we both laughed together. I am amazed that he allowed me to discover my strengths in such a supportive fashion. I remember asking him why he let me take those chances. He told me, "Well, why not? You turned out all right didn't you?" I doubt I would have the confidence to let my children risk a fall, so they would learn to walk better. I would need to run to their rescue.

My own son and I took a similar trip up north. It was not as rustic a visit as years ago. I was a little more cautious about walking off on the trails. I may have been holding back the trust that my Dad had been willing to give to me in the same circumstances. I know I would not allow my son to lie to get his way, as I saw so many people do in my teenage years. Yet, there are also many similarities in my method of raising my son. I have been satisfied with less for myself for the sake of my children. I was determined that my children have the opportunity to go to college. I trusted my children to make the right decisions, and I have the expectation that they will do their best. My father said it well, "Testing may not be the right measure of intelligence. The success of a man is how happy he becomes." I try to stay young at heart, not afraid to play the "goofball" with my son at times, yet remaining his father in authority and example. I remember asking my mother how my own father measured up to the stresses of a job where he was demoted for sticking to his principles in the face of pressure. She told me, "Oh, he is a master at it."

Today my son has developed a passion for scuba diving. As I reflect on my father's lessons to me, I intend to encourage and to support him directly by becoming his diving partner until a peer fills in when he is eighteen. I can see a close relationship developing in that choice. I hope I can change even today to be a more effective, more trusting and more cooperative father to him. He tells me he wants to drive out West when he graduates, and I think, "Oh boy, here we go again. He's heard that story, and now I'll only have a few years to develop the same trust my father offered to me." It may not be that hard a task after all. Last year his teacher showed me an essay in which he had written: "My Dad knows everything!" My son has often been able to come to me first, to ask questions where he could not figure out answers for himself. I am told his peers refer to him as the class role model. That fills me with great pride as his father. I know I will not fail to develop a more grateful spirit, especially when I see such a grateful heart in my son.

## *The Secret of Success*

*A father would consider himself successful if his son grows happy and healthy. He has even greater reason to be proud when his son becomes a caring, non-judgmental and supportive man.*

My times were so different than my father's experience of life when he was my age. Hardship and meager resources were not things that were easily replaced with the hopes of prosperity. I remember his thriftiness on many occasions, perhaps recalling his past, "careful lest the bad times return." Adults of my childhood tended to be gatherers and savers, much quicker to rush to a bargain or clip out a coupon. The number of their peers had been seriously cut by the ravages of war, and even though there was a new population boom, hence the Boomer name, there was a noted hesitant approach to life that only close family ties and greater family production could eventually resolve.

I grew up on a small family farm. We raised dairy cattle as our main means of support, augmented by crops to be gathered in the summer and fall. My four brothers and I were held accountable by my father for the many chores which contributed to the success of the farm. There were also fun times of baseball twice a week, frequent riding of my bicycle to visit friends who were neighbors and the satisfaction that came from knowing that any problems in the world did not seem to touch me or disturb the order of my family life. I learned from my Dad's expectations that I was to carry out my responsibilities of work until the task was completed. There was an order to life. Dad labored on the farm, Mom organized the home, and we were expected to take advantage of the educational opportunities offered to us. As the middle child of five siblings, I was marked out for further education.

When my aptitude for mathematics and science became evident, Dad encouraged me to consider an eventual engineering degree. I was excited about such a prospect and never considered anything else.

Movies and television of the time seemed to show us the great turning point of our country in the post-war years. The media spoke to me of the world being ours and that our new generation would be expected to decide what to do with it. My father's words to me were only an encouragement, "The sky is the limit for you. You can accomplish anything you want to!"

My father was generally a quiet man, and had expectations of how we were to behave, and he encouraged us to take the initiative. It was not uncommon for him to spend time with us, take us for rides, drive us to get ice cream or to go swimming at a nearby lake. His interest in us made our lives pleasant, yet he did not share much about his childhood. He was not hesitant to use harsh words if he decided I was not doing my best job. I recall one day he came out to the barn to discipline me for my tardiness. "You were late starting," he said with frustration. "I won't tolerate this laziness any longer. And speed your pace up. You're slowing us all down!" That was enough for me to change my attitude.

The year I left to go to college, he decided to sell the cows and take a job as a custodian, which at the time would assure a better income. This also diminished the farm work considerably for my two younger brothers. They were left alone when their older brothers had set out on their own. His decision rather surprised me, as Dad often said he was not able to do work other than farming. He had lost his left hand in an accident before I was born, but that disability did not stop him from doing any farm activity. By the time his family had grown up, it seems he began to believe even his lack of a hand would no longer prevent him from taking advantage of opportunities off the farm. Obviously his new employer had agreed. He was successful in that job and enjoyed his life for another ten years until my mother's tragic heart attack and death at the age of 65. Unstoppable, he eventually remarried and lived with his new wife for another twenty years until she also predeceased him by five years.

I know I have learned from my father the principle of being a good example for my son, participating in his activities and encouraging him in his education. I have tried to instill in him the integrity of a day's work for a day's pay. He has become a real gentleman, taking my values to the next level and with help from his mother, has perhaps become more refined than his father. When he was a child, I tried to encourage him to use his talents to pursue his ambitions. I remember the hockey game when he scored his first goal. I was the typical hockey father. I was angry when he received a penalty and I left the rink to cool down only to miss his eventual triumph. Even though the team lost that game, I encouraged him, "You should hold your head up and congratulate the winners. You should be proud you did your best. I know I am proud of you!" He cheered up. "We'll win the next one," he told me.

My son has grown a great deal since that day. Today at twenty six he has a degree in neuro-physiology where he monitors brain activity during operations. He hopes that he can become a doctor, and I say if he wants to do it, he can. I have no doubt that he is able to make the sacrifices to succeed.

It was the birth of my first child that was a pivotal point in this Boomer's life. With that little life in my hands, I understood the need for a stronger faith, a trust in God and a spirit of thanksgiving for all that I had. If I was to expect this child to do what was right, to grow as a person of integrity, I needed to be part of a system of faith. My father's system of protection was one based on his fears of failing his family.

There was always the chance that someone else would get ahead and beat my father to the chance he needed to succeed. I neither have that fear, nor have I passed on that fear to my son. Both of us know the value of a bargain; and in fact, I have seen him be quite frugal, living on a small amount for a long time. He is never short on friends and people who will be more than happy to employ him for occasional tasks. In fact, I was always insistent that he cultivate good friends. I may have been more critical than his mother, but I know he understands I want him to excel in whatever he does. I was particularly moved and proud to see his response to his best friend's brain injury. Left with permanent brain damage, his friend had to be taught again even the most simple of tasks. The boy's father tells me the good job my son is doing in aiding the slow recovery of his friend. My son's response is to say very little about it, but he continues being a very caring and committed friend.

I am happy to say that we, too, have become friends. As an adult, he does not need me to be a disciplinarian any more. His departure from home in a few months will return my wife and me to an empty nest, and I will miss sharing with my buddy the hope that our favorite team will again win the Series.

I worry a little about the unrest in the world, the terrorism and why people continue to hate each other enough to threaten each other with wars and death. My family has come from the Depression Age into the Cold War Age to the Terror Age, but I never hear my son focusing on those miseries. He reflects upon his desires and hopes in a more happy-go-lucky fashion that I wish I could recapture. He occupies himself helping those around him in a very caring profession. I know I have played some small part in teaching him to treat others with respect and to apply that necessary Golden Rule: "Do unto others as you would have them do unto you!"

Free from the prejudice that infects our society, he has come to respect the individual and not make his judgments on any other factor. That is reason alone for me to be assured of his future success.

## *More than Living for the Day*

*A father may give the impression to his son that he is only occupied in the here and now. Yet, he wants his son to be focused on his own goals. He encourages him to do that by supporting him but not by being his only means of support.*

The first time I heard the words "Baby Boomer," I was in high school. My teacher told the class that we were part of a great generation and that we would be remembered for our large numbers. There was no worry at that time that maybe that number was going to be too big to eventually support itself in retirement. For me, the 1960s was a progressive time. I do not remember having many worries, and my parents did not seem to be overly concerned about the racial unrest or the assassinations occurring in the decade. Life for our family revolved around whatever occurred in our neighborhood and in the nearby town. We lived for the day, and my father had no problem providing us with a decent lifestyle. Our home was on a small lake, and as we lived outside the city, our experiences tended to be rural in flavor. When I was seven years old I discovered the game of golf. This pastime has continued as a lifelong passion. I was able to play on my father's country club membership whenever I wanted. In those days no one ever questioned why such a young lad was regularly on the course. My two brothers and I eventually worked there as caddies, and later we cared for the grounds. Even though I am a teacher now, the summer months provide an opportunity for me to work again at that same course, grooming the greens.

I was the middle son of the family. We were raised in a home that was loving but strict. I listen to parents talking today about their experiences in disciplining their children, and I am surprised how big a difference forty years can make. When you attempt to discipline your children nowadays, they might look at you as if you have no particular authority over them. Some even refuse to comply and get away with it. In my day, if you disobeyed a teacher, you were not only fully disciplined at school, but you had a second dose administered when you returned home. There was generally that kind of mutual support among adults in the raising of children. Today many parents attempt to support their child without discipline and are often lacking in modeling discipline themselves. Such was not the case in my childhood home. My mother was a strict disciplinarian. She did not threaten us with the classic "wait until your father gets home!" She had no problem in handling such issues herself. Further, she was known by the neighbors and appreciated by one and all as the "drill sergeant" of the area. How did the young people feel about it? Maybe they were annoyed at the time, but I can tell you that they learned to love and respect her. It was with great emotion that I saw many of them present at her funeral in 1987.

Dad, on the other hand, had the skills of quiet leadership. He moved from Rhode Island after earning a Master's degree in engineering from Harvard. By 1957 he invented the pleated paper element and the adhesive process for oil filters. He made a name for himself, as was typical for inventors of the time working for a big company. The owners paid him two dollars for the patent and no more than a good pat on the back and a "well done!" Later, he was able to move to the sales level of engineering and this promotion made a more flexible schedule possible. I often watched him working with prototypes, and drawing sketches, long before the days that computers made the process so much easier. He was able to come home from work by 2:00 p.m. each day. Upon entering the house, he would yell to my mother, "If anyone calls, I'm not home!" His experience in the field told him that his products sold themselves, and he was able to spend more time those afternoons "tinkering," as Mom called it.

One of his greatest pleasures was teaching us to play golf on what he referred to as "the family course." When he told me, "Let's go!" I knew what that meant. We headed for the closet, picked up our clubs and were out the back door. He enjoyed teaching the game to his sons and watching us become more proficient players. Even when it was obvious we had surpassed the level where he could teach us more, he did not let that dampen his enthusiasm.

When we were a house of teenage boys, our parents let us come and go without much fear or control, as long as we lived up to our commitments did well at school and finished occasional tasks that they asked of us. I followed a similar tactic with my sons. Even in this age, the method seems to have been successful. My two brothers and I graduated college, and I predict the same for my three children.

My father never bragged about his many accomplishments. I found out much later that he had finished high school when he was sixteen and college at nineteen. When he was not accepted at the Naval Academy because of his eyesight, he settled for joining the navy and participating in a three year deployment around South America. When he left the navy, he returned to college and graduated with his Master's degree from Harvard. He did all of this before he had turned twenty five. He had married at twenty but waited another fourteen years before starting a family.

I was married at twenty six and did not wait as long for my three children. My son seemed to grow like a whirlwind. Whenever I asked him to do a task, he always had the ability and insight necessary. I coached him in soccer for six years, and he would just walk out onto the field and perform whatever play I suggested. Of course, golf played a large part in our time of bonding. Much like my experience with my father, he also has skills that surpassed his Dad. I remember my father not being as interested in my sporting or extra-curricular activities, as he was intent on my grades being the best. As my son enters his senior year in college, he tells me that he wants to be a coach. Since he has a clear vision of how to carry out an instruction, I believe he will be successful encouraging his players to develop this kind of skill.

I have tried to instill in my children that they can count on me but not become dependent on me. Money is usually the focus for this kind of lesson. I have been more pro-active than my wife in that area as she tends to want to lovingly give them what they want. "Perhaps you can earn the money for that yourself," I tell them. "In the real world you pay for things. Welcome to the real world!" I am more than glad to help them out by signing to support a small loan but to pay for everything is not in my plan for parenting. "You have to live your own life more and more," I told my son when he expected me to pay for the last item on the wish list. "You cannot just hang onto your mother and me." I want them to know that the world is open to them and hope they will go and experience it!

When I was twenty three, my mother developed Lou Gehrig's disease. Her illness continued for three years. My father would not let us help him in her care and made it clear to us that this was his responsibility alone. Her death crushed him and caused him to retreat into his own depression. A year later my older brother was diagnosed with pancreatic cancer. His death within twelve months increased Dad's depression to the point where he began living like a hermit. He has just recently started to return to the world after thirteen years. You would never guess he is 88. Despite all the tragedy he has experienced, he still maintains a youthful appearance. I have always strived to focus on and appreciate the people who are around me today, and not to live in the past. Living this way makes me happy and is not as stressful as a life dedicated to making plans for the future.

The illness and death of my mother helped me mature. I realized that my parents would not be there forever. I was able to make a commitment to my future wife, search for a better job, and start a career and a family. My Dad tried to help me to avoid the mistakes he felt he made in life. I needed to experience my own path so that I could make my own decisions. I appreciate that more fully as my own children travel their journeys and I can see what may be ahead for them. I'm always tempted to let them just live for today, but I find myself saying, "Don't sit back. I wasted too much time settling down before I was able to reach my goal. Be more like your mother!"

My son is a more outgoing person than I ever was. He is beginning to focus on his goals. He knew from the beginning that he wanted a college education. I think he will be successful. "The energy for your success comes from what you have dreamed about," I tell him. "Don't worry about trying to please us in your decision. Please yourself and be a success!" I have come to realize that I can fully appreciate the day and still look forward to what is yet to come. I am looking forward to the joy my son will offer me as he makes his life choices. There will always be more golf and I intend to enjoy teaching the game to yet another generation.

## *Life Lessons That Come From Fathers*

*It is interesting to note how many sons tend to quote their father's idioms. They seem to recognize the wisdom even when they find the moral difficult to embrace. Wisdom, like the lessons of life, is a gift a father can offer to his son.*

I'm a rather late Boomer, born close to the end of the generation. My remembered experiences began in the 1960s when I was a teenager. It was an age of destruction. We, the young, were encouraged to do whatever felt good and to accept a culture where drugs were available Society did not yet seem to cry out against these excesses. This experience arrested the emotional development of many of the youth of the age, and as I tell my son, "The drugs centered your concerns on yourself and you would stop growing up."

My own home was a safe harbor from the toxic culture around me at the time. My father worked a nine to five job; my mother stayed home and looked after us. We ate the family meal together each day, and we celebrated a rather happy family life. I was the eldest of four children, two boys and two girls who lived in a one thousand square foot, middle class home with our parents and my grandmother. My father took great enjoyment in our summer vacations. His goal was that our family would visit every state in the contiguous United States, and he succeeded! Our annual trek consisted of pulling a trailer behind the car and stopping to camp each night near the sites we planned to visit the next day. In the summer weeks that we were at home, I enjoyed playing in the neighborhood parks where young people in the immediate area would gather for baseball and other forms of recreation. As I entered my teenage years, the neighborhoods began to change. School funding became restricted as a result of the decreasing population and down turns in the economy. School hours were limited to half days and there was less contact with the teachers. Families that had lived in our neighborhood for years began to move away. My father reacted to this threat to our family's security from the change in our community by following their example. He decided we would move farther away from the city and into a more rural setting. Dad had grown up as a country boy in rural Tennessee and yearned for the days when his family had an orchard and a garden. He did not delay in creating all he had hoped for when we moved to our new home. He has continued to live that dream to this very day.

Dad believed in paying for everything with cash, and he did that when purchasing his new home. He was able to afford such a move as the new area was a much cheaper place to live. One of the first memories I have after our arrival in our area was a visit Dad and I made to the nearby university town. Sitting with him in an outdoor café we witnessed a 1960s style feminist protest. Aggressive women marched down the street past the café, waving brassieres in the air and screaming a loud chant. I asked him, "What was that all about?" "Finish your drink, we're headed back home," he growled.

But Dad was never slow to teach me lessons. I grew tall at a very young age, and I towered over most of my friends and all of my family. I never considered how a tall person could intimidate by his very presence in the room. I remember when I was nearly ten that I was in a fight with my brother, and I nearly ripped his arm out of its socket. My father locked me in my room alone for two hours. When he finally appeared at the door, he spoke forcefully and deliberately, "As of this moment there will never be violence with anyone in your family." He closed the door behind him. I think a great sense of responsibility in caring for other people took hold in me that day. The years that followed included serious consideration of the plight of those who are in need around me. I participated in a youth work program for the poor in Mexico. I volunteered in a nursery, taking care of babies when their mothers were attending C.P.R. classes for their newborns. I tutored handicapped youth in mathematics. I never considered before that time that those children, whom I saw as quite normal in appearance, could have such difficulties learning.

Dad also impressed upon me a great and necessary respect for women. "Treat every woman like you would your mother," he told me, "or don't interact with them at all. If you wouldn't say it to your grandma, don't say it at all!" I knew where he had learned this. He had been the only boy in a family with five girls. His father never treated his mother well, and many times he had to physically come between his father and his mother. He never wanted to see his sons repeating the actions of his father.

He further taught me about how to handle conflict when I accompanied him on a trip to check on my grandparents' former home. Dad was in charge of collecting the rent. The renter was a manic depressive. Upon our arrival, he became abusive and threatening, throwing punches wildly. I watched my father duck and sway, never being hit, but never hitting back either. This was a man who had understood conflict and fighting. He had enlisted with his best friend on December 8, 1941, the day after the attack on Pearl Harbor. On the way home I questioned him, "Why didn't you defend yourself?" "Violence never solves anything," he responded. "It only leads to you becoming a violent person." This lesson, like many he taught me over the years, I have never forgotten.

I always say that my two boys are fortunate in that they have been influenced by a good mother. She wanted to have good sons more than successful sons. I first met her in our workplace, and I knew immediately I had found the woman who would be my wife. It took me four years to believe I was worthy of her and to muster the nerve to express to her how I felt. I proposed to her on our first date. She must have thought I was undisciplined but not enough that she was unable to say yes to my proposal after six months and "I do" at our wedding a year later. I remember how her younger brother, upon seeing my beard, rushed home to tell his parents that their daughter was dating an old man! But her parents reacted to me well. Her father told me, "If you can accept our large family and put up with our home movies, you are already part of the family!"

I told my oldest son before he left for college, "The most important decision you ever will make is choosing the right person to marry." We had been watching the choice of girlfriends by our sons. My wife has her own way of screening the candidates, although so far no words have needed to be spoken. The boys seem to always choose the girls who exhibit great intelligence!

I've watched and learned an important parental skill from my father: Never discipline your son when you are angry. Like Dad, I have learned to step away and cool off rather than strike out in anger. If I act otherwise, I am in danger of destroying the chance to remedy the problem. During those two hours I was banished to my room, I was able to conjure up a much more understanding and just image of my father! If my children were to see my reaction as one of anger and punishment, they would learn that this is how men and fathers approach conflict.

I believe that marrying younger than my father did has given me a few more years to be active with my sons. While Dad taught me to hunt, he was unable, because of his work schedule and eventual pains of age, to continue hunting with me. I hope my strength will hold out so that I may be able to share in my sons activities for a long time.

I remind them of what I have learned often myself, "You become the person you pick as a friend." I'd like to believe I have been that good friend to them as well as an example of good fatherhood. May all their choices lead them to become the good people their mother always encouraged, and the good sons their father always supported.

# FOLLOWING IN MY FATHER'S FOOTPRINTS

The preceding twenty eight stories were composed by the author from data provided from personal interviews of men from the Baby Boomer generation. It was not the author's intention to make each text a biography, but rather to express the age using the voices of Baby Boomers.

Common experiences emerged from the stories of Boomers. Reflections on those experiences are indicated below to clarify for the reader critical aspects of the Baby Boomer era that affected these men and influenced their lives. As they became fathers, their experiences were passed on to their sons through their parenting. Some of their generalizations about life during this period include:

- Baby Boomers are so named because they belong to a large population of children born during the rapid and prolonged surge in births which occurred after the end of World War II, when so many fathers returned home and began building families.

- The home was established by a father who was the breadwinner and a mother who did not usually work outside the home.

- The father was often a strict disciplinarian and the mother received emotional support from him in her daily care for the children.

- There were usually several children in each family, involved in such group activities as eating meals together, growing produce in a family garden and playing baseball with the neighborhood children.

- Parents often stressed the importance of education and supported a teacher's right to discipline their children.
- There often existed a great respect for authority.
- Families knew their neighbors, and discipline was also maintained with their support.
- Many parents were immigrants to the U.S.A. who had a strong work ethic.
- Parents had been deeply affected by the Depression and often were thrifty savers.
- There was more face-to-face contact before the rapid advances in communication technology.
- In the early years of television, viewing time and frequency were minimal in comparison to later years.
- Lives were impacted by the invention of conveniences and labor-saving products creating more leisure time.
- The 1950s were a prosperous, slower-paced time. Danger no longer loomed on the horizon; a period of relative respite followed the terror of the war years.
- In contrast the 1960s were years of upheaval, defined by the race to the moon, the Cold War, the Cuban Missile Crisis, the Kennedy assassination, and the assassinations of Robert Kennedy and Martin Luther King, race riots, the Vietnam war, the feminist movement and political protests.
- In light of the above, Boomer children of the 1950s had a different experience growing up than did the Boomer children of The 1960s.

- There was a steady population migration to the suburbs from city centers.

- The growth in population led to increasing concerns about healthcare and the environment. At the same time, it created a generation more intensely focused on self and the "me first" philosophy.

These common elements in the history and experience of Boomers would affect lives and was passed on to their children. Inasmuch as Boomers could see the effects of the Depression and immigration on their own parents, so could the Boomers own children recognize the influence of these two decades on the lives of their parents.

These vignettes of the experiences of Baby Boomers are neither all-inclusive nor complete in scope. They are offered so that the voices of the respondents can be heard and general reflections from their unique perspective might be offered. Relationships are often complicated and can be difficult to understand from outside the family experience.

May the voices of these men of various backgrounds offer the reader a broader view of the Baby Boomer experience, and may they help subsequent generations of sons better understand the forces that shaped their father's lives.

William J. Turner is a Roman Catholic priest, pastor and associate professor who has earned doctoral degrees in theology and cultural anthropology. The son of immigrant parents, he developed early in life a love for family, ethnicity and cultural environment. Today, he researches and writes with passion on the effects of change upon men and women of the current era. He advocates respect for the identity expressed by his many research participants. An avid believer of anthropological methodology as a resource in understanding the experience of the individual, he promotes listening to and respect for cultural identity. Before change and growth can be adequately accepted, he strongly encourages the reduction of a forcible agenda, which has been so often present in proposals for renewal and reform.

# A FUTURE BOOK ABOUT FATHERS

## In My Father's Path

Fathers in their senior years look back on their experiences with a distinct philosophical approach to the father and son relationship. A more spiritual emphasis has entered into their stories as they bring to conclusion such concerns from their early years as heard in *In My Father's Steps* and the mid-life reflections related in *In My Father's Footprints.* Their stories and dialogue help readers understand not only the lives of these men, and how they have arrived at a place of peace, but also encourage all fathers as they advance in years to understand the true value of their fatherhood and sonship.

*In My Father's Footprints* is the second in a three part series on father-son relationships, having been preceded in 2005 by the collaborative effort *In My Father's Steps.*

*In My Father's Steps* is still available on line by contacting *theleanstore.com or writing to MCS Media Inc., 888 Ridge Rd. Chelsea, MI 48118.*